Real Estate Investment Trusts

Development, Successful Management, and Transactions

James A. Boyer, M.B.A., Ph.D., D.C.H.

VANTAGE PRESS
New York

FIRST EDITION

All rights reserved, including the right of
reproduction in whole or in part in any form.

Copyright © 1992 by James A. Boyer, M.B.A., Ph.D., D.C.H.

Published by Vantage Press, Inc.
516 West 34th Street, New York, New York 10001

Manufactured in the United States of America
ISBN: 0-533-10085-2

Library of Congress Catalog Card No.: 91-91296

0 9 8 7 6 5 4 3 2 1

If a thing is true at all there is a way in which it is true, and when the way is seen, we find that to be perfectly reasonable which, before we understood the way, appeared unreasonable.
—Judge Thomas Troward

Wisdom is a Tree of Life to them that lay hold upon her.
—Book of Proverbs
Chapter 3

Contents

Table and Charts	vii
Foreword	ix
Preface	xi
Acknowledgments	xix
1. Introduction	1
General Introductory Statement	1
Statement of the Problem	10
Importance of the Study	16
Limitations of the Study	17
2. Review of the Literature	20
Reading Sources	20
Working Bibliography	21
3. Methodology	33
Method Used to Study the Problem	33
Published Factual Data	34
Observational Data	36
4. Findings and Results	40
5. Summary	48
Appendix A	51
Appendix B	59
Bibliography	119

Table and Charts

Table I	23
Chart 1: Approval Capital/Borrowed Capital	53
Chart 2: Start-Up Capital	54
Chart 3: Growth Capital Combined	55
Chart 4: Rise/Peak/Fall/Rise Viable Reits	56
Chart 5: Cumulative Interest	57

Foreword

If there were ever a timely book—even overdue—in the field of finance it is this one! Dr. Boyer, who is a conscientious and thorough researcher, has brought the history and possibilities of Real Estate Investment Trusts (REITs) into the approaching twenty-first century. No one with any interest or knowledge of real estate trusts can fail to be impressed by this outstanding work—and *profit from it*. Almost daily, new scandal, failure, and even tragic stories of loss are reported in the press. Much of this could have been avoided by following the guidelines so clearly developed in this excellent treatise.

The subtitle of the book, "Development, Successful Management, and Transactions," is not in error—Dr. Boyer does just what is promised in the subtitle. The book deals with an enormous amount of data (all pertinent and clearly explained), but the emphasis is quite rightly placed on the beginning of REITs and the demand of the general public to invest money in a financial vehicle that would give a return larger than could be obtained through other financial institutions.

Dr. Boyer describes the style of management and the specialty of that management with regard to investments and the acquisition of funds. There is constructive criticism of much of the personnel in charge of investment funds and how many moved beyond their areas of expertise and abilities. Dr. Boyer doesn't just criticize many in the management of REIT funds but is most constructive in making recommendations for correction in this matter.

Dr. Boyer clearly demonstrates how the lack of proper supervision and poor advice led to the demise of many outstanding REITs and the loss of billions to the investment community. Dr. Boyer has answers!

There are many muckraking books in this area as a result of the economic tragedy that came to many in the REIT investment field. However, this book is not of that caliber. It is a considered, thoroughly researched text with many constructive suggestions and recommendations. Too, the book would be outstanding in teaching students concerning the entire history, planning, and program for REITs—it would be an outstanding text for developing a very sound and economically viable real estate investment trust. I commend the book to anyone with an interest in finance and real estate investment trusts in particular.

> JACK H. HOLLAND, MBA, Ph.D.
> Emeritus Professor of Management (1948–79)
> San Jose State University

Preface

This examination of real estate investment trusts emphasizes the methods, philosophies, and physical restraints encompassing the organization of equity real estate investment trusts, debt/mortgage real estate investment trusts, and combination real estate investment trusts.

The author combined and modified two diverse organizations—the equity real estate investment trusts and debt/mortgage real estate investment trusts—into a totally new financial instrument, all-encompassing in every respect, new organizational structure, philosophies, and modified physical restraints.

As founder and chairman of the board of this project, the First National Realty Trust, First National Advisors Group, First National Investment, Inc. (1977–present), the author provides a history, statistics, the development, and model of the trust documents, approved format, and a discussion of the marketing stages toward a finalization and fruition of the thought, substance, and results of the undertaking.

Real estate investment trusts were perceived initially as an exemplary approach for investment enhancement and an organization that would successfully meet the public demands for enlargement of a specialized segment of basic societal needs, real estate funding, pooling society's resources, creating a greater source of funds through which the public could share in growth, both of ownership and profits, independent of individual management.

Real estate investment trusts were enacted into law, authorized and established by Congress, in 1933–34.

The Securities and Exchange Commission was charged with the guidance and control of publicly traded securities and stock exchanges. Additionally, other major entities who offer guidance and control are the attorneys general and the corporation commission of each state, who have review privilege regarding sale of all stock issues advertised, marketed, or sold within their respective statutory areas whenever the stock registration is under the jurisdiction of the Securities and Exchange Commission.

The Banking Acts of 1933, 1934, and 1935 were enacted by the congressional majority, establishing the trust entities as one of the newly approved financial instruments to act as conduits of funds, thereby creating responsive organizations with legal authority to invest the society's capital in real estate activities and enhancing the opportunities of the achievement of much larger developments than singular capacities could accommodate.

This book sets forth the problems and responsiveness to the manifold variants and constraints of the responsible financial organization's path, diversity of goals, and methods of achieving the demands of investors.

As a study of an experimental project that provides a service through debt/mortgage financing and also providing a service through equity ownership within the full scope of a diverse public environment, the review-and-comparative method was utilized.

Simplification of this approach was accomplished by reviewing the development charts, policies and procedures, philosophical and restraint statements, visual pattern displays, and hosts of other banks from the many sources available, all of which are public documents.

Data of every conceivable magnitude are published quarterly by the individual trusts and are available to the general public. Copies of the quarterly report are delivered to their respective investors, stockbrokers, attorneys, the Securities and Exchange Commission, and other listed departments of all levels of private and institutional agencies.

These reports are called prospectuses. Within each of these individual prospectuses the trust lays bare all pertinent and factual data regarding their individual organization's progress—good or bad.

This system has merit, as it provides only verifiable facts and figures, and it eliminates any opportunity for inaccuracies in presentations.

Other referenced information is published daily, monthly, quarterly, and annually in newspapers, magazines, journals, and association manuals, including reports directly from the federal government printing office.

A compendium of information is published by the National Association of Real Estate Investment Trusts, Inc. (NAREITS),[1] under the heading of *Handbook of Member Trusts 1974–1975*.[2] The findings for this dissertation are based upon those published, documented, factual and historical data compiled through resources within those publications and other public documents within the public library system that refer to the 164 member trusts active and members of NAREITS at that time. Other documentary data are from my own personal library.

These reports, documents, and firsthand knowledge represent the major sources of data and information contained herein.

The author accepted the opportunity to attend major and minor national and international conferences at which the total thrust and intent was to ascertain the problems and to develop solutions through peer experiences, utilizing training seminars and relearning basic business principles and concepts.

The staff and panels of these conferences were beset and bewildered by the various conflicting philosophies and physical restraints imposed on the successful and the not-so-successful membership trusts, both internally and externally, of the overall association's membership.

Analyzing the data of the 164 trusts with references to the individual trust needs and association and investor demands, the results of these analyses support so many areas of disruption that crisis policies and procedures were initiated by necessity to save the total collapse of the whole group of real estate investment trusts as individual viable organizations and as members of the National Association of Real Estate Investment Trusts, Inc.

The individual entities were ill-equipped at this stage of development to manage the tremendous explosion of resources (capital), organizations (people), and scope (territory) that became available to them. Although normally and ideally this phenomenon should have benefited each entity involved, it is the author's findings and opinions that actual results revealed instead an impending disaster, which caused an upheaval that culminates in the destruction of approximately 75 percent of the real estate investment trusts association membership.

Rules and regulations established internally, according to organizational philosophies, and externally by the Securities and Exchange Commission, combined with public demands under the authority of law, fueled this inferno by forcing developments of real estate–oriented projects to be funded, purchased, and ventured, wreaking financial havoc on the independent, untrained, and unskilled literate and illiterate in financial management in young organizations.

Real estate investment trusts come into a physical entity—an organization—by two primary philosophical concepts. Management philosophical concept in the equity trust is markedly displayed by the majority of resources held and invested in ownership of the project's assets. These ownerships extend for indefinite periods, generally not less than four years. The other philosophical concept is the debt/mortgage trust, which directs the energies of the organization toward funding short-term and long-term debt/mortgage instruments.

Equity ownership is not a usual occurrence in debt/mortgage trusts; likewise, debt/mortgage financing is not generally the expertise located within the equity trusts.

The securities that are sold are called shares of certificates of beneficial interest. This name is explanatory of the actual ownership and method of that ownership. Trustees of these trust organizations hold in title in their personal name as trustees the actual ownership of all assets. The investor capital is represented by the certificate of beneficial interest denoting the percentage of beneficial interest within the trust's total portfolio.

The sale of trust securities (certificates of beneficial interest) is processed through the many stages of governmental regulations prior to actual advertisement through prospectus distribution. The Securities and Exchange Commission requires registration, including any state governing bodies charged with the securities' registration and review.

These securities, after all requirements to market the securities are satisfied, fall within two categories: (1) private placement of the securities and (2) public sale through the stock exchanges.

Stock brokerage houses market the sale through the stock exchanges, offering the securities to be sold as shares of certificate of beneficial interests.

Similarly with other organizations that market their securities to establish minimum purchasing quantities, a policy is established to decrease the number of shareholders, thereby decreasing the administrative costs of the movements of funds and paperwork overhead.

The actual sale of the securities of trusts, when properly marketed, takes place within a very short span of time, ranging from minutes to a few hours.

Trust regulations are established to allow for a minimum of one hundred owners of shares of certificates of beneficial interests to validate the compliance with the law. The minimum number of shareholders must be satisfied for the trust to remain a viable real estate investment trust.

The second method of funding the trust is private placement of the securities. This method takes place by two avenues of securities—the exchange of shares of certificates of beneficial interests for real estate-oriented assets with a combination of cash infusion for the remaining securities or an outright investors' program that acquires the securities.

Other financing vehicles available through institutional organizations allow for leveraging and borrowing capital. The intended purpose of borrowed capital is to fill any gap of short-term or long-term funding requirements.

The securities of real estate investment trusts are dissimilar as to the redemption and sale technique via mutual funds securities in that mutual funds organizations provide a total market for any number of securities of the various funds' shares. The real estate investment trusts organizations do not; trust securities are only traded on the stock exchanges or private placements directly from the trusts.

These methods of funding may be different, but both of the methods—however unique—must comply with the same regulations as set forth by the governing agencies.

The requirements of both types of trusts specify that quarterly documents and other data that may be required by the Securities and Exchange Commission must be published.

Both styles and types of trusts are considered to be closed-ended in terms of the quantity of securities' representatives of shares of certificate of beneficial interests. Certain amounts of securities are approved, when sold; additional purchases are acquired through the exchanges through the investors' respective brokers.

Generally, a new issue for the sale of securities for trusts will be made available but once a year.

Buyers and sellers create their own market. The price of the securities is usually established by the price/earnings ratio, i.e., the costs of the security versus the return of interest that the buyer perceives as a future asset. The culmination of the marketable securities is generally referred to as a free market or free enterprise system.

Real estate investment trusts receive funds from the sale of shares of certificates of beneficial interests less cost of sales. These funds that are received by the trusts eventually are invested in some type of real estate project less overhead costs of the trust organization. The investment of funds develops the portfolio either as equity/ownership asset or as a loan to an outside borrowing entity denoting debt/mortgage asset or as a venture partnership, combining the several formats of the contractual requirements available encompassing those necessities that the venture project demands.

The management astuteness in performing these roles and intricate actions combine the essence of the purpose, intent, and goals for which the trusts were established.

These roles/actions of managing investments require both short-term and long-term funding obligations creating the financial instruments that the management of the organizational trusts were obliged to coordinate.

These funds were from a combination of the public earnings, savings, gifts; all funds, however entrusted, were exchanged for shares of certificates of beneficial interests for the sole purpose of profitability in the use of their funds.

Funds entrusted to the management of the trusts were disbursed by contractual obligations in which the trusts had previously been entered into with various entities, through controlled policies and procedures established by the management of the various trusts.

These policies and procedures, when not strategically developed, planned, verified, and finely honed, inevitably started the erosion that was to develop in resultant losses of both principle and interest income, thereby eliminating the intent of the investor-entrusted funds.

The ensuing fallout resulted in the destruction of approximately 75 percent of the real estate investment trusts' members failing as a viable organization, thereby causing discontent, discord and, finally, withdrawal of society's support in this specialized market.

To be commended for their astute business acumen in both management and investment policies are those managers of sixty-plus real estate investment trusts held among the remaining 25 percent of the member organizations. Historical documentation lists those who survived the downward spiral.

The results of the failed real estate investment trusts prompted this author toward a conclusion of consolidating thoughts, substance, and results.

Targeting the project toward the establishment of a new financial instrument, a new style organization, and a more unique form of philosophy included a modification of physical restraints that could combine and withstand the combinations of pressures of internal and external expansion and contraction modes.

This new instrument and organization structure, found in chapter 5 of this book, should extend the roles and actions of the new philosophies and modify the physical restraints toward a more diverse infrastructural support vehicle.

The misperceptions of investors and trust management causeded both internal and external failure to meet their respective goals due to the many-faceted problems that became the downfall of their respected financial domains.

Verification of the published data of each faltering project and trust's responsiveness tended to be entirely different than perceived by management and the investment communities.

In summary, the author contends that the flexibility of the trusts, potentially as an asset, actually was the cause of the special circumstance that maneuvered the organizations into the ills of the 1970s.

The obvious problems clearly demanded a solution, and the issues were addressed. Of paramount importance was the organization of more highly trained and skilled staff, operating within the framework of an expansive philosophy, which included a modified physical restraint pattern mandating corrections that eventually emerged.

New styles of organizational precepts were designed, and the new organization was termed a combination real estate investment trust.

The combination real estate investment trust came into existence in 1977 for several purposes, one being to assist in shoring up the poorly performing existing trusts as a model for those trusts that were not proving themselves successfully.

This book sets forth a compendium of data illustrating those changes incorporated to form a combination real estate investment trust, leaving the equity trusts and the debt/mortgage trusts intact, and it will add another dimension: the third financial instrument in style, form, and type authorized in real estate investment trust organizations.

The combination real estate investment trust documents, as herein presented, are today a model for the industry.

Notes

1. National Association of Real Estate Investment Trusts, Inc. (NAREITS), 1101 Seventeenth Street, N.W., Washington, DC 20036.
2. Edited under the direction of G. W. Buffington, Executive Vice President and General Counsel, National Association of Real Estate Investment Trusts, Inc.

Acknowledgments

I wish to acknowledge and state my deepest appreciation for support from the following: my children, Randy, Rick, Donna, and Chris, and my very best friends and exemplars, Mrs. Margaret Barrows and her daughters, Jean and Carol, who have encouraged me toward completing my doctoral program.

I wish to acknowledge those tremendous and remarkable studies, lectures, and training at the Church of Divine Science, El Toro, California; the Reverend Jean L. Murphy, D.D., Minister/Director, in association with Jack H. Holland, Ph.D., D.D., Professor Emeritus, School of Business Management, San Jose State University, California; Frank William Varese, M.D., Director, Health Associates, Laguna Hills, California; and one of the great illumined giants of our time, the late Joseph Murphy, Ph.D., D.D., LL.D.

Real Estate Investment Trusts

1
Introduction

General Introductory Statement

The Great Depression of the 1930s affecting the United States as well as engulfing the remainder of the world nations was bursting at the seams of discontent, failures mounting through every segment of business and agriculture, including the total monetary system, all in the embryo stages.

Results of these major problems were creating strife, hardships, and mistrust throughout each segment of the national economy, including employment, banking, industry, and trade—both domestic and foreign. A drastic and necessary modification of securities affecting the national monetary system was recognized and addressed.

The New Deal administration responded to the challenge under the direction of a newly elected president, who was charged with the responsibility of the reorganization of priorities, a functional program, and new leadership toward bringing to fruition a new and viable productive system for our nation. Correcting the future roles and functions of all segments of the economy was, indeed, a monumental task.

New and dynamic methodologies were developed by the New Deal administration. These newly perceived plans/programs were expanded into suggestive legislation. The executive branch of government requested the House of Representatives and Senate to pass into law, called acts, the requested legislation.

The dynamic driving force toward developing new policies and procedures was the president and the newly appointed cabinet members, who requested the Congress to pass these newly adopted concepts toward the attempt to correct the nation's economic ills, which changed the course of short- and long-term events.

The securities area affecting the overall monetary system was one of the first major legislative efforts for the administration to address. The securities market was in total disarray, and it was of paramount importance that it be completely reorganized and brought under control of the federal government—substantially for reasons that the securities funds act as a conduit of investment capital for the national economy.

The new administration recognized the need to reestablish a sound monetary system. New policies were established through the authorization of laws with the passage of acts by Congress that provided society with new banking regulations and insurance of depositors' capital, including a new regulatory body.

The newly formed organization, called the Securities Commission, was charged with the responsibility of regulating all securities when sold on the stock exchanges. The authority that allowed for the new commission to develop the administrative power and to control the securities nationally was ensured by the Securities Act of 1933. Following within a year of enactment of the Securities Act of 1933, the Congress enacted into law the Exchange Act of 1934.

The determination of the different time spans of these two legislative acts was basically political in nature, the brokers not desiring any control by the government over the securities even though the estimates of sales of valueless securities were exceeding 50 percent of the marketplace transactions.

The exchanges were necessarily brought under control to prevent churning, reselling the identical securities to the same group of investors several times. Those illicit sales were not requiring deposits of funds, thereby creating a marked increase in sales activity. The brokers, in total control, sold the securities for their respective brokerage houses and clients at the selected top of the market. The original investor paid nothing for the stock and accepted a fortune for the use of the name. The brokerage house received its commission, and the program was repeated consistently.

As a point of interest, the names that were prevalent in this program through 1929 and the 1930s are again appearing in the exchanges' transactions of 1987 and 1988, all representative of great moral philosophies.

The Securities Commission and Exchange Commission rapidly came under the control of one single commission, called the Securities and Exchange Commission in 1934.

New legislation creating a new system of depositor insurance was heralded in 1934, with a newly formed corporation called the Federal Deposit Insurance Corporation. This new Federal Deposit Insurance Corporation was charged with the responsibility of developing guidelines for the protection of depositor funds by all banks that were then members and under the control of the Federal Reserve Board.

Initially, only those banks that were members of the Federal Reserve Board were authorized to join in the subscription of insurance for the banks' investor capital. This requirement was later dropped, allowing for all banks to purchase and to acquire the insurance program upon meeting the guidelines as established by the Federal Deposit Insurance Corporation.

The name is truly a misnomer in that these two organizations are not part of the federal government. Both are private organizations, funded by the many banking institutions national in scope. After a number of years, beginning in the 1980s, the president of the United States, assisted by the Economic Council staff, shares a 50 percent role with the chairman of the Federal Reserve Board. The Federal Reserve Board is composed of a select few bank chairmen and presidents of the oldest, largest financial institutions.

The Banking Act of 1935 expanded the role of the Federal Reserve Board, thereby enhancing opportunities to expand throughout the national monetary system.

The Federal Reserve Board, the Federal Deposit Insurance Corporation, and the Securities and Exchange Commission, working independently, form a triad of powerful agencies affecting the entire nation.

Other commissions, boards, and corporations were also established for the purpose of controlling, administratively, each segment of the major national and international marketable industry. To name just a few, in addition to the earlier mentioned agencies there were the Railroad Commission, earlier established but with an expanded role, Federal Trade Commission, Labor Commission, Agricultural Commission, and Federal Communications Commission, to develop some insight as to the envelopment of control over this nation's economy.

Each agency acknowledged the responsibility to promote and control the specific area of its authority, all of which were under the direction of the New Deal administration.

The Federal Reserve Board, responding to their first order of business, successfully achieved the goal of stabilizing the many bank failures and closures. This was accomplished by providing a regulatory system of borrowing capital from the Federal Reserve banks.

Regional Federal Reserve banks were established in twelve selected areas of the nation. The Federal Reserve Board member banks throughout the nation were assigned to one of the twelve regional Federal Reserve banks.

The reopening of the entire nation's banking system was accomplished by a proclamation of the newly elected president as of 6 March 1933.

The Federal Reserve system was previously established in 1913 and was totally administered by the privately owned Federal Reserve Board, made up of member banking institutions.

In conjunction with the Federal Deposit Insurance Corporation, they developed numerous approaches to develop memberships in the entire private banking industry under the Federal Reserve Board's auspices. Numerous privately held banks and state banks staunchly refused the membership invitation. The Federal Deposit Insurance Corporation amended their bylaws and adopted a new stance that permitted the Federal Deposit Insurance Corporation to function with member banks and non-member banks under the guidelines as established by their insuring corporation. In 1939 the total banking industry was formally approved to be insured under the control of a privately financed and owned national body.

The banking industry, administered by the Federal Reserve Board, drafted new controls, simultaneously instituting new policies and procedures, especially in the lending procedures, cashing of debt instruments, checks, deposit requirements, transference of securities, gold and silver deposit minimum reserve, and an accounting and auditing control procedure.

The goal of the Federal Reserve Board was to enlarge the monetary base of the member banks, including the national network of banks, for the establishment of an all-inclusive monetary trading facility throughout the nation.

Prior to the New Deal administration, the various states and private industry controlled the banking/financial field with little direction or administration review by federal governmental agencies. The Securities Act of 1933, the Exchange Act of 1934, and the Banking Act of 1935 were approved by Congress, which provided a momentum of power, direction, administration, and control previously unknown to this nation's enterprise system. It was the beginning of an evolution.

The new commissions, corporations, and boards were established to direct and influence the area of their objectives within each segment of the economy through interaction by the use of the holistic approach. Each commission, corporation, and board wielded great power and answered only to the New Deal administration. The power of decision as to which segment of the economy was allowed to expand or contract was included; the resulting fallout, of course, meant disastrous results to those caught up in a spiraling decline and a profit for those caught in the growth trend. This style of manipulation follows the same pattern today controlled by this same triad led by the Federal Reserve Board and its management of the economy for the nation.

One can visualize the procedure: at the request and suggestion of the administration, Congress passed the recommended and requested new laws, modifying others for greater control; the commissions, corporations, and boards applied the laws summarily, subject to answering only and responsible to the originating governmental body that enacted the new laws.

The Securities and Exchange Commission's primary responsibility was two-fold: correcting the stock exchange method of operations and regulating the registration of securities of every conceivable nature, on a national basis.

The very broad scope of authority resting within the parameters of each commission, corporation, and board was impressive. The Securities and Exchange Commission, through a national public demand, caused by the upheaval in the stock exchanges and securities transactions, was forced to the forefront of this embattled area of discontent, powerfully wielding all their authority necessary to force into law new guidelines and requirements. The new laws set the trend in a direction of total control of the securities industry, toward areas of investments with specific goals, for micro-economic growth and macro-economic growth parameters.

These goals, well-intentioned and thought-provoking, were established by all commissions, corporations, and boards, elaborating their desires to withstand the expansion and contraction that was necessarily desired to control the nation's economy.

The entire arena of securities registration and sales and the stock exchanges' transactions, less one of notable size, that being the futures market contributing most of the activity to the Chicago Exchange, now lies totally within the management, authority, and guidelines of the Securities and Exchange Commission, their authority vested within the Exchange Act of 1934 and the Securities Act of 1933.

The banking industry's previous approaches to business transactions had become extremely diversified with lending policies ranging in magnitude of ultra-conservative toward inflationary exhibitionism.

These extremes of the activities of banking transactions diverted many bank clientele, former investors, both large holding companies and frequently the junior investors/customers from the banking mode.

This group of investors had two major purposes: control of their assets and a fervent desire for profitable management of their funds. Seeking avenues to create such an entity, pressures were applied, in accordance with the securities laws and banking rules, on the Securities and Exchange Commission. The Securities and Exchange Commission, responding to these pressures and requests, approved the creation of a new instrument and style/type of organization including the authority to sell securities, and hold and manage investors' collective funds and resources. The new entity was named real estate investment trusts.

Trust, as an entity, was on the public scene many years prior to the development of the real estate investment trusts. Trusts are one of the very important administrative functions in the armory of management tools. Trusts were instruments of the national financial scene, holding enormous wealth under its control; to name a few: individual, corporate, public, industrial, and service trusts. All were established to administer their own assets and invest their capital as their own management directs.

The one particular style and type of trust instrument and organization specifically dealt with in this book is the real estate investment trust. The authority to approve this new trust rests within the broad scope of authority within the Securities Act of 1933 and the Exchange Act of 1934. The new commission was named Securities and Exchange Commission in 1934.

There was a twenty-eight-year span without the approval or formation of the first real estate investment trust, which could be traded publicly through the stock exchanges or over-the-counter exchanges or as a public entity.

On May 25, 1961, the Securities and Exchange Commission authorized the first real estate investment trust that could actively trade stock on the stock exchanges and the over-the-counter exchanges. First Mortgage Investors Trust was the first of a series of trusts to follow. First Mortgage Investors Trust was originally capitalized with $15 million.

Thereby the Securities and Exchange Commission succumbed to the public pressures mounting within the securities parameters and approved the development of a specialized organization to service one of the basic industries—the real estate industry.

The public's desire was to invest their savings in an organization that would invest their cumulative funds on a much broader scale than was then available within the individual investor locale.

The choice to join a larger group and to pool their resources under management of a specialty organization was then available in two styles and types of real estate investment trusts. These two trusts were described by the philosophies from the trustees of the trust and the management of the trust funds by the contracted advisory organizations. The trusts were aptly named equity real estate investment trust and debt/mortgage real estate investment trust. The combination of the two philosophies of management established an additional style and type named a combination real estate investment trust.

In defining the roles of the two parallax organizations, equity real estate investment trusts were authorized to spread the investors' capital/shares of beneficial interest throughout the nation, purchasing ownership of those selected projects and thereby becoming an asset of the trusts. The accumulation of assets then became the total equity trust's portfolio representative to the investor as a value of their stock, namely, certificates of beneficial interest.

The ownership of selected projects encompassed the full range of types of projects. The percentage of ownership also varied, with some having total ownership and others a limited ownership, all based upon the contractual agreements of each project.

The equity real estate investment trust owners, holders of shares of certificates of beneficial interest, were paid dividends of the trusts' activity, which included the sale of assets, rental or lease, or lease-back's income, and which then passed through from the trusts to the stockholders of shares of certificates of beneficial interest without capital gain taxation of the funds by the trusts' accumulation.

The tax consequences of those profits that were distributed are taxed as individual taxpayers' defined tax brackets. This method of investment, management, and ownership was very passive, heartily accepted as a boon for the investors' motives.

The opposing style of philosophies was named debt/mortgage real estate investment trust. The trustees and advisory groups professed a philosophy that extended the owners of shares of certificates of beneficial interest invested resources into a lending mode—no ownership—namely mortgages, both short-term and long-term mortgages, junior mortgages, gap loans, intermediate term, development loans, standing loans, and overlay or wrap-style loans.

The profits of this style of management trusts were also passed through to their investors (holders of shares of certificates of beneficial interests) and taxed in a like manner as the equity trust participants. The earnings were from interest on the invested capital primarily. There are a few other income sources in each of the trusts that are received—to mention a few, standby fees, commitment fees, loan fees, servicing fees, origination fees, and appraisal fees. Some of the fees are in excess of the overhead costs and leak into the profit structure occasionally.

Foreclosures on loans affecting the borrowing entities are a major source of revenue and occasionally a source of revenue loss, the loss revenue directly attributed to erroneous appraisals. The revenues earned on foreclosures and the resale of those assets or leased assets creating excess income are also passed through to the individual holders of certificates of beneficial interest.

Both equity trusts and debt/mortgage trusts were required by law to be disbursed and pass through to their shareholders of certificates of beneficial interest in an amount equal to at least 90 percent (currently 95 percent) of their net profits annually to remain qualified as a real estate investment trust. The remainder of 10 percent (now 5 percent) is taxed as corporate capital gains under the laws of the Internal Revenue Service.

The obligations that were placed onto management of the trusts were solely and purposely established, forcing the trust management to remove and distribute the income—namely, net profits—annually.

This obligation carries with it a matching disruption of the trust's liquidity, leaving the trust totally invested in hard or extended liabilities with little to no capital to satisfy future investment obligations. This disbursement method created capital expansion shortages.

Because growth is vital to all business enterprises, compression of the trusts resulted in management-desired need to make available capital in which to satisfy their desired goals. Additional debt type/style of borrowing was initiated other than the originally intended format of selling shares of certificates of beneficial interests on the stock exchanges and over-the-counter exchanges.

Initially, short-term borrowing was the solution to the capital-short enterprise. Certificates of deposit were purchased and used as a portion of the security of the borrowed capital from banking institutions. Notes, secured and unsecured, lines of credit among one or several banks, mortgages, and commercial paper were the outstanding methods of borrowing directly from banking institutions.

The available capital in the expansive mode that was propelling the nation was not competitive and/or in short supply relative to the enormous amount desired.

The trusts turned to the marketplace again. In a few cases new shares of certificates of beneficial interests were sold; most, however, were not marketed to the public but to institutional lenders who prefer to invest in an instrument, namely debentures. This tended to be the trend through 1973, with its significant beginning in 1969.

All the funds were intended for the purpose of maintaining a growth pattern equating to the philosophy of the trust management and the demand of the investor; secondarily, for the retention of their ranking in total assets accumulated; and thirdly, to develop a price/earnings ratio based upon the volume of dollars invested and increased income to challenge other competitors, thereby holding, and it is hoped, adding new investors' capital investments. The approach appeared basically optimistic—basing the premise upon volume of investment of dollars into inglorious projects, hopefully always producing the best results. Consequently, the Price/Earnings Ratio (P & E) did suffer, causing the direction of the real estate investment trusts to turn to institutional investments, all with a guaranteed return, most with several options for additional investments if the trusts performed satisfactorily.

The Securities and Exchange Commission permitted and allowed the establishment of two types of trusts, each diametrically opposed as an organizational and financial entity in competition with the banking industry's investment policies and programs. These diametrically opposed organizations, by design, created philosophical and physical restraints. Within those parameters, both operated as such through the 1960s and 1970s, during all of which time the majority of real estate investment trusts directed their energies toward a multiplicity of individual goals.

In the early stages of development, few real estate investment trusts made a niche for themselves until the early 1970s, at which time "real estate investment trust fever" broke out from among the many financial institutions, likewise with new entrepreneurs in the investment field who were vying for a public vehicle–style organization, one that would allow the diversification of the institution funds as well as the entrepreneur funds as a method of expanding their existing portfolio on a broader scope.

Chart 1 (see Appendix A) displays the approval volume and period of build-up for the trust organization.

Chart 2 (see Appendix A) displays the start-up capital cumulative of all trusts in the various years of funding.

Chart 3 (see Appendix A) displays the growth and ending capital of the cumulative trust assets.

The interim period of real estate investment trust development was rife with havoc, as overexpansion and contraction and interaction within the infrastructure of public -requested demands, resulting in faulty planning within the advisory groups and in the approvals of those ill-conceived programs by the trustees of the real estate investment trust, placed the real estate investment trust into a financial tailspin, thereby creating a domino effect beginning in the year 1975, some fourteen years from their inception.

Statement of the Problem

The collapse and ultimately the failure of real estate investment trusts were moving the majority of real estate investment trust association members toward a national disaster, forced upon the organizations by philosophical and physical restraints. The rules, regulations, strategies, and planning were totally out of control.

The current hypothesis is the question of how the real estate investment trusts are to avoid similar entanglements in the future and should naturally begin with the problem of how, in fact, they got into this debacle. In confronting the future, the first guide is the experience of the past, which frequently is misleading. The experience of the 1960s and 1970s has the defects of many historical experiences.

It is confusing and baffling to the extreme. The deceptive simplicity of the facts conceals a tangled jungle of motives, of conflicting economics and psychological influences, of unstable assumptions as to their proper basis of organizational action or the nature of the society's process.

It is not difficult to describe what happened by the references of the compendium of data available. When the real estate investment trust complex of organizations totally exploded in the latter half of the 1970s, the shock to the nation's economy was almost as violent as that of investors' emotions. The situation was in both respects something with which real estate investment trusts were totally unprepared to deal.

Real estate investment trust development as an organization and the flow of events that occurred in the establishment of the trusts typically flow through the following format.

Effectively, the trust, as a real estate investment trust, does not gain approval as a trust until a number of specific functions are accomplished and reviewed by many authorities, the last being the Securities and Exchange Commission, prior to the sale of shares of certificates of beneficial interests to the public. Initially, there must be a body of interested parties, institutions, or individuals who are proposing the establishment and who also wish to pay the billings insured in this endeavor. The costs can mount from a low of $200,000 to $750,000, depending upon the costs of legal, accounting, advertising, overhead, administration, and other start-up fees. These costs are somewhat universal in the industry in which the author initially considered somewhat over-inflated awaiting the final tab of costs in the preparation of a trustee's outline in chapter 5. Please believe the costs; they are very factual.

Finalizing the documents, as outlined in chapter 5, one then proceeds to locate a brokerage house that will underwrite the sale of securities; at the same time the projects in which the money or newly acquired funds are to be allocated must be available, utilizing 90 to 95 percent of the new funds' investment final journey.

Sponsors of developing real estate investment trusts have in the past accomplished the goals within a year; generally a longer period is the norm.

After the basic organizational formation is completed, a certified public accountancy firm is contracted for the future certifications of the accountancy of the trust's operations.

Following closely is the contractual hiring of a major legal firm or firms. The two service organizations are of utmost significance, and the decisions on the two should be respectful of some definite research on the part of the sponsoring groups.

The advisory group and the board of trustees are truly the management corpus of the trust functions. The importance that the sponsoring entity places is a direct representation of the longevity, purpose, and profit proliferation of responsibility that eventually overshadows all other functions previously described. Consequently, these positions must be filled with straight-line thinkers of the highest caliber who can think of quality, not necessarily quantity, for one can rest assured that the opportunity for success multiplies dramatically. If not, it will assuredly falter just as dramatically.

The trustees, natural or legal persons to whom property is legally committed to be administered for the benefit of a beneficiary, are an elite group inasmuch as they hold personal title to all the assets of the real estate investment trust. Theoretically, they make all the major decisions, set the policies and procedures into motion, sign all the contracts, and hire all the staff personnel. In effect, they represent the titular head of the organization. These trustees generally are astute in many facets of business acumen with proven results over many years of experience. Abdicating and relegating their responsibilities appears to be a major element of failure of those organizations in the late 1970s.

The lineal organizational positions are staffed as requirements build—usually a skeleton base initially, then expanding in number as funds and projects develop. This development did not occur in significant numbers, allocating the usual positions to outside contractual organizations. However strong an argument one wishes to pose for this method, it certainly didn't work for 75 percent of the real estate investment trusts.

The advisory group is a licensed group of select individuals who are under contract to the trusts. Their responsibility is to locate new quality projects and present their suggestions and recommendations to the board of trustees. The method of paying for the services is possibly a culprit that the trust industry should review.

The method of payment is a percentage of the gross invested assets of the trust funds. This may abridge the quality of responsibility, tending toward quantity over quality, expansion over conservatism. Greed could possibly have crept into this system. However, none of the original advisory groups was changed through the period of 1961 through 1973 based upon the finding of this research. Even though the contractual period was for a one-year span, it was renewable only upon successfully providing a service that the trust organization required. In a few cases, the advisory groups were the representative organization of the sponsoring trusts, thereby also a significant number representative on the board of trustees.

Stock brokerage firms are generally selected by past performance and most generally share with other brokerage houses in the marketing and sales of the shares of certificates of beneficial interests to selected clientele and to the general public.

Banking institutions, by their very nature of purpose, are an integral part of the monetary system and play a very important role by holding in trust accounts the funds that are generated from the sale of stock through the stock exchanges, transferring the funds to the final destinations in the account of the trusts.

Registration of the shares of certificates of beneficial interest is another function that has in the past appeared as one of their functions. New organizations have now sprung up to compete in this market.

It is essential that all these functions are well-coordinated prior to the funding of the real estate investment trusts. In accordance with a rule of the Securities and Exchange Commission, the majority of the funds are to be allocated immediately to specific projects for maximum return and not held in a trust account, unless under contractual obligation, for some indeterminate purpose or time.

The foregoing is the mundane exercise that is the forerunner of the day of sale—the day when the sponsoring organization finally sees the fruits of their efforts and fortitude in the seemingly never-ending problems and the corrections thereof and the wholesome expenditure of the sponsor's funds.

Sharing some of the future excitement is the sale day of the shares of certificates of beneficial interest. Stock exchanges open early for the West Coast operations. One arises early to attempt to acquire the latest sale figures on the trust offering. The sale of the shares can be made within minutes or a day. The time, however, can appear an eternity. The call from the brokerage firm confirms the sale of the total offering; bank accounts bulge from a zero balance to the millions of dollars. All signals are go. Projects that are previously assigned funding resources need final contracts signed by all parties; checks are written and accounts balanced, inspections are called for and finalized, quarterly reports are scheduled to begin, and computers with a varying degree of output come on line. Excitement reigns, new problems arise, training starts, and there is more training, and more funds arrive that need investing. A new set of priorities is required—which project?—and so the days and weeks become a little longer, a little more hectic, as the challenge manifests itself and new requirements press forward.

I have intentionally placed the foregoing paragraphs into this book precedent to the following statements.

In effect, this is one of the very few businesses that have a zero bank balance one day and have millions of dollars in funds the following day. The trusts are expected and required to be fully operational on the day of the sale. A real estate investment trust must be accomplished and managed correctly to ensure success from the first day.

However unrealistic this may appear, new trust organizations have developed as such approximately 350 times to date since 1961.

These processes are not impossible; they are proven to be justifiably practical and successful even though they are dramatically unusual in the financial world, particularly among newly formed businesses with the successful proviso of such a broad range of services.

Initially, inexperienced personnel were placed in positions of authority. Management later found this to have been a grave mistake. It is hoped they have opted for the more highly experienced and adequately trained staff to function, whether contractual or staffed, toward a wholesome, successful operation.

Having had the opportunity to view firsthand the successful and unsuccessful internal decisions and their followup, this author appreciates the problems inherent with real estate investment trusts but also can relive the joyous occasions of the more fruitful, productive experiences.

As in all businesses, a few notable experiences teach one rapidly, painfully, and thoroughly to recognize quality opportunities when and as they appear. It is also of prime importance to recognize those elements that contribute to the failure of the vast majority of real estate investment trusts during the past fifteen years. Following are areas of special concerns illustrative of typical causes of unsuccessful real estate investment trusts.

In a number of encounters with the trust staff personnel, notable areas of problems appeared and reappeared.

Mortgage loans were activated by the trusts in various areas of the nation totally illiterate of the demand, demography, without totally engineered drawings or permits. Adding to these problems, they had not utilized any significant time to review and analyze the projects that the funds were proceeding to build or allocate for short-term or long-term mortgages. In numerous cases the funding was a direct response of a contractor or a contracted institution located in distant areas of the nation.

The contractor selection was also a giant of a problem that tended to raise its ugly head ever so many times. These problems can be linked directly with lack of inspections or allocated budget control. Expenditures more than exceeded the project's progress. Need I take you to the end of that morass difficulty?

Lack of funding control was the paramount problem of the inexperienced, illiterate lending specialists in the field of construction. Mortgages were being foreclosed for many reasons, but one factor was most predominant: the income stream was not sufficient to service the overhead and mortgage requirements. The foreclosure action positioned the real estate investment trusts with either a deficit monthly income balance or zero income, depending on the legal sequences that followed the foreclosure. The majority of cases awaited new lease arrangements through evictions of the non-paying occupants. Thus the management of the trusts were honored with the responsibilities not only as a debt/mortgage trust but also an equity trust for long periods of time too numerous to mention.

Manifold benefits are derived from a well-managed and adequately funded trust and are well worth the considerable investment of time, effort, and preparation. These benefits extend into the public arena, providing a broad spectrum of production.

Problems, yes. A complement in excess of twenty-eight thousand staff employees was within the business of trust management for the sole purpose of tracking progress of funds and maintaining control of developed assets, all of which assets are trusteed resources.

The advisory groups to these trusts, which were under contract as a service organization, employed approximately 25 percent of the twenty-eight thousand, which may indicate a ratio of staff in trusts to contracted advisory groups. Numerous trusts contracted the services of such advisory groups that one normally associates with a corporation organization.

The banking industry gained a new financial associate, a borrower, a great depositor, a joint venturer, a client who had the financial clout to remove the bank from long-term obligations, and finally a great organization that pays interest payments on time and in large numbers, this obligation through tremendous borrowing instruments.

Public resources were created and numerous employment opportunities were offered. The enhancement of goals was achieved in private housing subdivisions, new schools, and new roads, new and abundant funds flowing into the economy, which multiplies their good in so many quarters of our nation.

Governments—local, city, county, and state—all benefited from these funds when used for newly planned master-planned industrial and commercial developments.

These represent just a few of the benefits and pluses that real estate investment trusts accomplish by consolidating funds and releasing those funds in well-defined bundles to provide funds for those creative programs that otherwise may not have found their path into fruition.

Importance of the Study

As beneficial as the trusts may appear, surprisingly, this author found only one doctor of philosophy among the total of twenty-eight thousand employees and no woman on any advisory board or board of trustees. This should be a very lucrative field for those qualified in the areas of management and administration. Real estate investment trusts provide an excellent opportunity with salaries commensurate with the responsibilities involved.

Real estate investment trusts definitely are specialized organizations, and that specialty obviously requires and demands a group of highly informed and trained personnel to operate within the framework of that specialty.

The boards of trustees and the advisory groups were exemplary in form and were heavily comprised of the financiers who were on the boards of the world's largest banks and other financial juggernauts, including a few from the world of real estate.

These groups with financial acumen undoubtedly sought the funds as a source for providing a path for fame not existent in the organizations of their existing havens. However mistakenly their roles were perceived, 75 percent failed in achieving success in those well-intentioned goals.

Whereas the real estate investment trusts are public entities, accountability of those funding policies is not responsive to federal and state regulation and scrutiny, as are the funds within the banking institutions.

Eventually this style of financing methodologies filled the portfolios of the many trusts with inferior loans, totally unbalanced. There was no partner to turn to. The interest payments and the principal became due with too little income to support the financial burdens, forcing the trusts into default. The investors became wary and no longer elected to invest in stocks to support these young organizations. The price/earnings ratios fell far below blue chip stocks. The result was a continuing erosion of new source capital to assist in correcting the course of events.

The final outcome of this debacle was the absorption of the weak trusts into the stronger. Those who survived were generally outside the management of inside influences.

A more encompassing instrument arrived upon the scene in the late 1970s to assist in relieving some of the problems inherent within the remaining trusts. This financial instrument and concept was named a combination real estate investment trust.

The author had the exclusive honor of developing the first documentation for combination real estate investment trusts, which was properly and aptly named First National Realty Trust. The initial funding offering is $50 million, illustrating the development of concepts, philosophies and physical restraints. This model, as displayed in chapter 5, will provide a complete compendium of data that may be used, with the publisher's permission, to develop real estate investment trusts for future sponsors, thereby giving back to the trust organization a service that will undoubtedly assist in the removal of time and money in future programs.

Limitations of the Study

The beneficial intent and purpose of this dissertation is to provide forty years of analytical and administrative data necessary for the successful achievement of developing a combination real estate investment trust.

The presentation of these views and a demonstration of expression consistent with the philosophies of each type of trust, including the physical restraints therein imposed, will efficiently and effectively function as a standard of public acceptance.

The nominal purpose is the correlation of the various views, which should pinpoint the variants, subjecting the organization to faltering when excessive demands are internally and externally imposed upon the trust organization and functions.

The overall program, as set out, focuses on the parallax views of trusts to present a new style of trust that will demonstrate the purpose, format, style, and type, creating and providing a service to the real estate investment trust industry.

Investment policies are the key in determining the philosophies and goals, including the physical restraints, that the board of directors (trustees) propagate as their purpose of the organizational structure.

A "current investment policy" would be presented in a typical statement as such:

> The XYZ Equity Investment Trust investment policy will be directed primarily to the acquisition of income-producing properties already constructed and occupied, but a portion of its assets may be invested in vacant land strategically located for commercial and industrial development. In making investments the trustees will seek stability of income and a balanced portfolio of sound real estate properties. The properties acquired by the trust may be located within or without the United States, meaning on an international basis, wherever the trust may legally operate. However, the trustees intend to invest in properties that are located primarily in North Dakota, southern Utah, and areas close to the city of Las Vegas, Nevada. The trust may acquire interests in real estate for cash, property, or shares of the trust. It will purchase properties for long-term investments and will not engage in short-term sales and purchases unless the nature of the particular properties indicates special reasons for believing that the proceeds of their sales might better be invested in other properties. Although the trustees currently intend to make investments in real estate only in the state of South Dakota, the trust may make investments in any state in which it may operate. The trust currently owns six investment complexes, with the option to purchase six more complexes that are scheduled for completion in June, July, and October 1989. The XYZ Trust's industrial complexes are located in Toad Frog, South Dakota, on Pondle Creek Road. The complex consists of a total of 6 million square feet of light industrial warehouses. Offices are included within each of the buildings. All six industrial complexes are leased. Leasing arrangements are for periods of five to twenty years. Other complexes are of the same design and are presently 60 percent preleased to AAA tenants.

Contrasting the equity trust with the debt/mortgage trust current investment policy, the following example illustrates the diametrically opposed view of investment and physical restraints.

The declaration of trust permits XYZ a broad range of mortgage and real estate investments that do not limit the proportion of the trust assets that may be invested in any geographical area. The trust's basic approach is directed toward achieving a diversified portfolio consisting of short-term, intermediate, and long-term mortgages. It invests an amount approximating its equity capital and long-term debt in long-term first mortgage loans and equity investments. The proceeds from borrowings are invested in construction, development, and intermediate mortgages. The types of loans and investments authorized by the declaration of trust are as follows:

First mortgage construction and development loans, which are short-term loans generally not exceeding three years and finance the construction of residential properties, condominiums, and income-producing properties. The trust may require a commitment from other lenders for the permanent mortgage before approving a construction loan. It is the intention of the trust not to advance more than 80 percent of the appraised value of the improved property.

First mortgage long- and intermediate-term loans consisting of conventional loans on commercial and industrial properties and on residential properties such as high-rise and garden apartment projects. Intermediate-term loans are normally for terms of three to five years, which are primarily for the purpose of permitting a developer to delay obtaining long-term financing in order to secure more favorable loan terms. Conventional long-term first mortgage loans typically mature in ten years, with twenty- to twenty-five-year payouts.

Other types of investments, including investments of up to 10 percent of the trust's total assets in junior mortgage loans. Wraparound loans are not included in this limitation. The trust may also acquire equity participants.

The combination real estate investment trust in chapter 5 includes the investment policies for First National Realty Trust.

The parallax views of the three basic trusts are representative of all real estate investment trusts that are available to the general public, all three with different views as a method to obtaining their philosophical goals within the constraints of the methodologies that will illustrate the corrections of course necessary to fulfill the investment portfolio's survival.

2
Review of the Literature

Few opportunities have existed or been experienced in the author's lifetime that exemplify a program as enormous as the development of real estate investment trusts, whereas one may view the paradoxical development of major entities in the business world today.

Organizations originating from an idea, a non-existent entity to a fully energized and funded entity, grow through the maturing and development stage only to collapse in total despair. Assigned to this calamity is a combination of philosophies of the many hierarchical organizations, culminating management's views within the newly developing organization's philosophies and physical restraints, which have been documented so well.

Reading Sources

Factual documentation—good and bad—producing a true compendium of events, philosophies, and physical restraints provides an expansive view of the entire public forum of real estate investment trusts.

One must appreciate the background, thoroughness of organizational structure, policies and procedures, trustees' business acumen, and staff of each of the trust entities, including management's scope of responsibility for those accomplishments that were heralded as successful. The author was paralleling the activities in searching for a logical definition of those areas that should be modified for achievement of success in the expanding market.

When the author was initially reviewing the published data and documents regarding the trust organizations, their objectives were illustrated in a context that would cause one to consider the newly formed trusts as a conservative method of investment practices, including formats of the principles of the philosophies of the trustees.

These principles of philosophies were documented in each of the debt/mortgage trusts and the equity trusts, furthering the logical conclusion that the trusts were truly self-sustaining through an expanding and contracting mode, thereby creating strong and viable organizations.

Underlying these newly founded organizations was a smoldering fire that was destroying the underpinnings of these troubled giants. This smoldering fire would eventually destroy their foundational support concepts. The inevitable fate was a decline toward failure and insolvency.

All the ingredients, including legislative authorizations, were in place for the young entrepreneurs with a new abundance of capital that few had experience to manage at the time of their mission, the unchallenged investment achievements, with the greatest velocity, toward unprecedented goals, as established by the trustees of the many trusts.

These goals were addressed by the numerous avenues of new project funding and purchasing for equity ownership. The totality of these opportunities projected the management of these trusts into a frenzy, a delirium of excitement, toward an attempt to invest at all costs in the presented projects.

The appearance of the policies suggested that few in the management decision process were spending sufficient time in analyzing the projects' future value, forgetting that excessive investment policies and borrowing techniques do not always produce the positive results hoped for. Lackluster use of skills became very apparent in their field of endeavor.

Working Bibliography

The published documents as filed with the Securities and Exchange Commission, including the quarterly trust reports, referring to a prospectus of the 164 organizations, were reviewed to ferret out the data producing these findings and opinions of the author, thereby creating a degree of credibility.

These lists represent those trusts that this author researched, documenting cumulative figures of their start-up capital, ending balance of assets, year of approval, and determination of whether the organizational philosophies were the debt/mortgage trusts (shown as D) or the equity trusts (shown as E).

These documents that make up these lists are approved by the trustees, legal counsel, and certified public accountants, including the staff of each trust organization.

The Securities and Exchange Commission has very effectively established guidelines specifically in the reporting process. Penalties, as outlined in law, cover a multitude of very effective sanctions and await those entities to make a demonstration of their effectiveness. Baring of the teeth of the Security and Exchange Commission will surely occur if data are presented incorrectly.

TABLE I

	Style and Type of Organization	Year of Approval	Start-up Capital (Millions)	Last Reported Asset Balance (Millions)
Alison Mortgage Investment Trust	D	1969	$18.6	$220.5
American Century Mortgage Investors	E	1969	26.5	185.4
American Fidelity Investments	E	1970	3.0	25.0
American Fletcher Mortgage Investors	D	1969	12.5	127.0
American Realty Trust	E	1961	5.0	51.0
Arlen Property Investors	E	1971	16.5	52.0
Atico Mortgage Investors	D	1969	15.0	111.0
Atlanta National Real Estate Trust	D	1971	25.0	47.0
Baird & Warner Mortgage and Realty Investors	E	1971	25.0	70.0
BankAmerica Realty Investors	E	1970	72.0	201.0
Barnes Mortgage Investment Trust	D	1972	38.0	84.0
Barnett Mortgage Trust	D	1970	20.0	299.0
Barnett Winston Investment Trust	D	1972	33.0	67.0
Beneficial Standard Mortgage Investors	D	1970	15.0	102.0
Berg Enterprises Realty Group	D	1972	13.0	27.0
Bradley Real Estate Trust	D	1961	5.0	21.0
Brooks Harvey Realty Investors	E	1971	50.0	50.0

	Style and Type of Organization	Year of Approval	Start-up Capital (Millions)	Last Reported Asset Balance (Millions)
BT Mortgage Investors	D	1970	$ 25.0	$154.0
Builders Investment Group	D	1971	60.0	331.0
Cabot, Cabot & Forbes Land Trust	E	1971	60.0	143.0
Cameron-Brown Investment Group	D	1969	44.0	158.0
Capital Mortgage Investments	D	1969	20.0	174.0
Central Mortgage and Realty Trust	D	1971	15.0	45.0
Chase Manhattan Mortgage and Realty Trust	D	1970	113.0	752.0
Chicago Real Estate Trustees	E	1980	4.0	4.0
C.I. Mortgage Group	D	1969	79.5	303.0
C.I. Realty Investors	D	1971	65.0	222.0
Citinational Development Trust	D	1970	12.0	29.0
Citizens Growth Properties	E	1971	16.0	40.0
Citizens Mortgage Investment Trust	D	1969	21.0	112.0
Citizens and Southern Realty Investors	D	1970	50.0	415.0
Clevetrust Realty Investors	D	1971	50.0	108.0
Colwell Mortgage Trust	D	1969	18.0	181.0
Commonwealth National Realty Trust	D	1973	15.0	26.0
Connecticut General Mortgage and Realty Investments	E	1970	120.0	446.0

	Style and Type of Organization	Year of Approval	Start-up Capital (Millions)	Last Reported Asset Balance (Millions)
Continental Mortgage Investors	D	1961	$23.0	$642.0
Corondolet Realty Trust	E	1965	5.0	10.0
Corporate Property Investors	E	1971	150.0	150.0
Cousins Mortgage and Equity Investments	D	1970	42.5	256.0
Cumberland Equity Trust	D	1970	.2	1.6
Delaware Valley Realty and Mortgage Investors	E	1971	1.0	10.5
Denver Real Estate Investment Association	E	1967	8.0	32.0
DeRand Real Estate Investment Trust	E	1972	.72	.72
Diversified Mortgage Investors	D	1969	154.0	364.0
Dominion Mortgage and Realty Trust	D	1971	6.0	27.0
Equitable Life Mortgage & Realty Investors	D	1970	150.0	267.0
Federal Realty Investment Trust	E	1962	2.5	28.0
Fidelco Growth Investors	D	1970	22.0	115.0
Fidelity Mortgage Investors	D	1969	40.0	277.0
Financial Florida Investors	D	1970	1.5	4.0
First Commercial Realty Investors	D	1973	23.0	63.0
First Continental Real Estate Investment Trust	D	1972	11.0	30.0
First of Denver Mortgage Investors	D	1970	30.0	104.0

	Style and Type of Organization	Year of Approval	Start-up Capital (Millions)	Last Reported Asset Balance (Millions)
First Fidelity Investment Trust	E	1969	$ 4.8	$ 28.0
First Memphis Realty Trust	D	1970	20.0	72.0
First Mortgage Investors	D	1961	15.0	558.0
First Pennsylvania Mortgage Trust	D	1970	38.4	150.0
First Union Real Estate Investments	E	1961	13.2	144.0
First Virginia Mortgage & Real Estate Investment Trust	D	1972	30.0	82.0
First Wisconsin Mortgage Trust	D	1971	30.0	30.0
Flatley Realty Investors	E	1972	8.4	25.5
Florida Gulf Realty Trust	E	1973	19.5	35.0
Florida Investment Trust	E	1967	5.0	6.2
Franklin Realty & Mortgage Trust	E	1961	7.5	47.5
Fraser Mortgage Investments	D	1969	18.0	43.0
Galbreath First Mortgage Investments	D	1969	16.0	70.0
General Growth Properties	E	1970	9.0	167.0
GIT Realty and Mortgage Investors	E	1969	11.0	41.0
Gould Investors Trust	E	1970	5.0	39.0
Great American Mortgage Investors	D	1969	26.0	413.0

	Style and Type of Organization	Year of Approval	Start-up Capital (Millions)	Last Reported Asset Balance (Millions)
Greater Western Real Estate Investment Trust	E	1972	$ 5.0	$ 15.0
Greit Realty Trust	E	1960	10.0	60.0
Guardian Mortgage Investors	D	1969	12.5	468.0
Gulf Mortgage and Realty Investments	D	1970	40.3	148.0
Gulf South Mortgage Investors	D	1971	15.0	33.0
Hamilton Investment Trust	E	1971	20.0	115.0
Hanover Square Realty Investors	E	1972	25.0	63.0
Heitman Mortgage Investors	D	1970	24.0	101.0
Hibbard, Spencer, Bartlett Trust	NA	NA	NA	NA
HNC Mortgage and Realty Investors	NA	NA	NA	NA
Hospital Mortgage Group	NA	NA	NA	NA
Hotel Investors, The	D	1970	22.5	73.0
Hubbard Real Estate Investments	E	1969	100.0	97.0
ICM Realty	E	1969	9.5	73.0
IDS Realty Trust	D	1971	60.0	127.0
Independent Mortgage Trust	D	1971	62.5	154.0
Indiana-Florida Realty Trust	E	1970	8.0	8.1
Indiana Mortgage & Realty Investors	D	1972	20.0	73.0

	Style and Type of Organization	Year of Approval	Start-up Capital (Millions)	Last Reported Asset Balance (Millions)
Institutional Investors Trust	D	1970	$ 40.0	$115.0
Investors Realty Trust	E	1969	22.0	61.0
Investors Reit One	ED	1968	5.0	14.0
Investors Reit Two	ED	1972	5.0	14.0
Investors Trust of California	E	1970	1.0	1.5
JMB Realty Trust	D	1972	10.0	20.0
Justice Mortgage Investors	D	1971	21.0	86.0
K.M.C. Mortgage Investors	D	1971	15.0	44.0
Larvin Realty and Mortgage Trust	D	1971	72.5	80.0
Lincoln Mortgage Investors	D	1969	22.0	50.0
Lomas & Nettleton Mortgage Investors	D	1969	27.0	350.0
Massmutual Mortgage and Realty Investors	D	1970	100.0	295.0
Mid-Atlantic Real Estate Investment Trust	D	1973	1.5	2.7
Midland Mortgage Investors Trust	D	1969	20.0	119.0
Miller, Henry S., Realty Trust	E	1971	10.0	32.0
Monmouth Real Estate Investment Trust	E	1968	2.0	9.2
Mony Mortgage Investors	D	1970	50.0	267.0

	Style and Type of Organization	Year of Approval	Start-up Capital (Millions)	Last Reported Asset Balance (Millions)
Mortgage Growth Investors	D	1971	$ 30.0	$ 51.0
Mortgage Investors of Washington	D	1970	15.0	110.0
Mortgage Trust of America	D	1969	63.0	177.0
M & T Mortgage Investors	D	1970	8.2	42.0
Murray Mortgage Investors	D	1973	7.5	17.0
Mutual Real Estate Investment Trust	E	1965	10.0	40.0
National Mortgage Fund	D	1968	4.0	69.0
National Real Estate Fund	E	1970	10.0	75.0
New Plan Realty Trust	E	1972	3.5	25.0
Newport Equities Trust	D	1971	1.84	3.9
N.J.B. Prime Investors	D	1971	30.2	98.0
North American Mortgage Investors	D	1968	43.6	244.0
Northern States Mortgage & Realty Investors	D	1972	5.5	31.0
Northwestern Financial Investors	D	1972	27.0	47.0
Northwestern Mutual Life Mortgage & Realty Investors	D	1971	100.0	179.0
Old Dominion Reit One	E	1972	1.0	4.2
Old Stone Mortgage and Realty Trust	D	1970	5.2	38.0
Palomar Mortgage Investors	E	1969	15.0	82.0

	Style and Type of Organization	Year of Approval	Start-up Capital (Millions)	Last Reported Asset Balance (Millions)
Pease & Elliman Realty Trust	E	1972	$22.0	$ 33.0
Pennsylvania Real Estate Investment Trust	E	1969	2.0	29.0
Philadelphia Mortgage Trust	D	1972	NA	NA
Piedmont Real Estate Investment Trust	E	1972	5.0	20.0
PNB Mortgage and Realty Investors	D	1970	36.0	135.0
Property Capital Trust	D	1969	30.0	73.0
Property Trust of America	E	1963	12.0	37.0
Real Estate Fund Investment Trust	E	1972	1.5	4.5
Real Estate Investment Trust of America	E	1961	11.0	42.7
Real Estate Investment Trust of California	E	1968	.448	6.3
Realty Growth Investors	D	1974	31.5	43.0
Realty Income Trust	ED	1962	6.3	66.0
Realty & Mortgage Investors of the Pacific	D	1971	50.2	78.0
Realty Refund Trust	D	1971	20.0	106.5
Republic Mortgage Investors	D	1968	33.0	91.0
RFI Realty Trust	E	1970	3.5	5.6
Riverside Real Estate Investment Trust	E	1969	2.0	14.2

	Style and Type of Organization	Year of Approval	Start-up Capital (Millions)	Last Reported Asset Balance (Millions)
Riviere Realty Trust	E	1963	$ 2.0	$ 21.0
Ryan Mortgage Investors	D	1971	6.3	17.7
Saul, B.F., Real Estate Investment Trust	ED	1962	7.0	301.0
Security Mortgage Investors	E	1969	30.0	218.0
Southwest Mortgage & Realty Investors	D	1971	5.5	17.3
State Mutual Investors	D	1970	60.0	99.0
Summit Properties	E	1965	.8	52.0
Sutro Mortgage Investment Trust	D	1964	2.2	91.0
Texas First Mortgage Reit	D	1971	21.0	63.0
TMC Mortgage Investors	D	1972	26.0	28.4
Tri-South Mortgage Investors	D	1970	27.5	215.0
Union America Mortgage and Equity Trust	D	1969	25.0	143.0
U.S. Bancorp Realty & Mortgage Trust	E	1972	25.0	46.0
United States Equity & Mortgage Trust	E	1963	.36	9.2
U.S. Leasing Real Estate Investors	E	1970	33.5	53.4
U.S. Realty Investments	ED	1961	6.6	141.0
Virginia Real Estate Investment Trust	E	1970	6.0	50.0
Wachovia Realty Investments	D	1969	61.0	190.0

	Style and Type of Organization	Year of Approval	Start-up Capital (Millions)	Last Reported Asset Balance (Millions)
Walter, Jim, Investors	ED	1972	$18.8	$45.8
Washington Real Estate Investment Trust	E	1960	3.0	31.6
Wells Fargo Mortgage Investors	D	1970	65.0	215.0
Western Investment Real Estate Trust	E	1964	3.7	7.8
Western Mortgage Investors	D	1964	4.8	34.0
Wisconsin Real Estate Investment Trust	E	1962	2.0	47.0

3
Methodology

Method Used to Study the Problem

The encompassing studies through research of individual trusts, their philosophies, direction of policies and procedures, and expansive modes of both organizations and funds, including the organizational structure, suggested a more in-depth study than originally intended for this book; however, the scope of research suggested valuable data not previously considered that has proven the findings and opinions as stated in chapter 1 justifiably accurate.

The research study did indeed produce several factors that figuratively produced a pictogram of related and unrelated propositional events that the author will describe in the following summaries.

The first and most attentive reminder of facts is that the trusts as a group were a relatively young organization; the formation of trusts was taking place over the last fifteen-year period, and the majority of organizations in this group were developed within the last five years.

The second proposition that was considered meaningful, thereby encouraging this study and adding some beneficial asset to the group's opportunities, was that it would be necessary for the author to join in concert with the trust organization.

The third proposition was that the subjects were a little-known study group and totally independent as a group, each operating as an individual entity with separate management and each maintaining its individual philosophical approach as to management styles, directions, and purpose, which permeated society's infrastructure.

This methodology and choice of involvement was that of action research—an observer initially, then as a participant for reasons of paralleling experience comparisons.

This style of research has an infinite number of subjective and objective qualities, allowing for micro-research to identify the subject's philosophical patterns of management, followed by an objective verification of the management's consequences through the results obtained.

The trust groups were small in number in relationship to the huge count totaling the sum of all business organizations throughout this nation.

The group, as published, represented the total membership of the national association of trust organizations, this group representing the most viable trusts, encompassing the total group membership nationally studied for this research.

There was a total membership of viable trusts numbering 164 as listed in chapter 2. The number of trust membership organizations enlarged the rolls following the published manual in 1975. The increasing numbers of new real estate investment trust organizations developed expanded the membership through the 1970s toward a peak just under 250, each viable with an entrepreneurial conquest.

Published Factual Data

This research sums the macro-findings as of the end of 1973 from the data available in the published reports.

A new and heightened surge of energy and interest was then coming to the forefront: external entrepreneurs elected to join this newly founded group. This new group, adding their membership numbers to the 1974 older membership roll, created a highly sought after, specialized merchant of their wares—money.

The major decline in trust failures had not truly begun when the data for this research were published, but the tremors of internal upheaval were being demonstrated both internally and externally.

The expansion of the economy tended to be the main reason for the expanding development and use of real estate investment trusts.

The aggressive growth of the economy and the expansion of the real estate investment trusts participating in the investment program of that expansion, ensuring issues of funding availability and interest, caused their demise, whereas the majority of real estate investment trusts faltered and remained viable for only a few years.

The expanding economy, prior to the mid-1980s, proved a boon to society. The expanding economy was challenged with new monetary guidelines reportedly brought on by the necessity of funding the military buildup and expenditures in the early 1980s.

These monetary guidelines moved the economy to one of contraction of economic growth by the fundamental use of interest escalation.

The policies of the Federal Reserve Board, a public entity composed of member bank officials who are appointed for varying years of service, which also is funded by the member banks with whom each of us transact our daily business, follow a conservative pattern of maintaining the economic health of the nation.

The Federal Reserve Board demonstrates the patience, intelligence, and control without allowing emotions to set the guidelines. These guidelines, however controversial, demonstrate to the investing consortiums that investing intelligently demands that we adhere to time-tested correct procedures and policies.

The five-year period following in the 1980s was a transitional climate from one of expansion to one of contraction. The main tremor that was to shake the industry occurred. The tremor, created by the economy and associated constraints, was excessively violent to the degree that newly formed trusts were unable to survive. A domino effect was to follow, affecting essentially the majority of the nucleus of the national association of real estate investment trusts.

The failure of these trusts was not an aberration resulting from external variants. The collapse occurred because the total management of these trusts did not know and possibly never did know what was happening, all clinging to their own philosophical approach, decision-making ineptness. Physical restraints adding to the dilemma were of unskilled management techniques.

A graph, as illustrated, will assist in the visualization of the numerical development of the trusts, the peak, the collapse, and finally the resurrection of this noble body of investment specialists. See chart 4, Appendix A.

It is noteworthy to remember that the percentages of all types of business failures remain consistently high. Over any selected ten-year span, nine businesses will fail and one will remain viable. The consensus of opinion as to the success of those remaining is the philosophical demands that were adhered to—that of patience, intelligence, and control of their emotions. Using this philosophy, their assets flourish.

The real estate investment trusts that remained, approximating sixty-five in number, as viable organizations of real estate investment trusts met all the requirements of the Security and Exchange Commission guidelines and represented an approximately 25 percent survival rate. The sequel to this book will attempt to uncover the basic philosophies that allowed for this higher survival rate.

The remaining trusts, reflecting the fittest, were then fortunate to be charged with the complexities of picking up the charred remains of a young, fragile industry that was perceived originally to have great resiliency.

Observational Data

The second and most significant area of response was truly the acid test that was conceived as a necessity, involving the author in their internal problems at several national and international conventions through a simple method of observation, listening to and debating the issues with management of the various trusts.

This technique was portrayed prior to attempting the research and writing of this book.

Reviewing the internal and external problems that were discussed at the conferences revealed a wealth of knowledge that one does not generally perceive while viewing the colorful exposure of the organizations from the outside.

These opportunities for the author to perceive the enormous problems in which they were groping and which were creating total havoc in a number of instances added to the author's personal experiences. He had previously encountered similar concerns, thus allowing for a discussion of experiences paralleling those of proven concepts to be shared.

Total management of the majority of the trusts was attempting to regroup due to philosophical direction and faulty management decisions.

The role of strategic planning was lacking in most organizations. These roles of strategic planning, if properly programmed with the correct data input, totally validated, surely will prevent the morass of complications that investment trusts have inherited. Isolating the future investment policies in a more intelligent manner will allow for management's energies to be expanded toward resolving the current dilemma.

Trust management directives were followed where those policies and procedures existed. This area of management responsibility should include moral philosophy, in the opinion of the author.

The funding of new projects was from leverage capital in the majority of transactions. This leveraging ability, when not held in check, created another weak area that allowed the posturing of the trust entities to mush and slide with the economy.

The marketing of new shares of certificates of beneficial interests was not consistent with the tempo necessary for allocating funding. The lack of new investor capital forced the aggressive management into a borrowing mode, obtaining capital from other financial institutions. This leverage borrowing of capital precipitated a higher interest rate to be charged to the real estate developers, much greater than desired by the many trusts, thereby placing the trusts in a highly competitive market for those few ideally qualified projects in which to place the newly acquired leverage and borrowed capital.

This identical program of borrowing is continuing to be advanced today, forced upon the management by law, which requires that income as earned each year must be distributed to the investment community. To be absolutely correct, 95 percent must be transferred to the owners of shares of certificates of beneficial interests.

The 5 percent of earnings remaining are taxed in a similar manner as a corporation. To relieve the double taxation, a distribution is generally the action taken. However beneficial this concept may be, the resulting operating capital is the remainder of capital after taxes and any returns of principal that are subject to mortgage repayments or sales of assets.

The author can understand the complexities of these requirements and appreciates the tax problems; however, numerous organizations of all magnitudes declare dividends and pay the dividend to the responsive investor only after future investment programs are provided with reserves of capital to accomplish the same.

This procedure, in the author's opinion, weakens the future role of real estate investment trusts, surely to be addressed as trusts mature.

The management has but three primary sources of investment capital: sales of shares, borrowing from financial institutions, and private placement. Removing the financial institutions as a lending source when interest rates are abusive causes the sale of shares of certificates of beneficial interests to generally evaporate. This dilemma is constantly repeating itself, forcing the trust organizations to be content with the market swings and long-term borrowing instruments at a negotiated (it is hoped) competitive rate.

Management's typical method of funding was borrowed capital. The methods of borrowing varied; however, the borrowed capital placed certain restrictions, including a return of the principal and interest on a scheduled basis.

This identical procedure was repeated time after time; the trust names only changed and included changes in the volume of dollars based upon the philosophical address of the funding needs for the trust projections, anticipating the requirements of future projects and allocation schedules.

Total management organizations were attempting to regroup from faulty management decisions, though they still lacked strategic planning and role modeling concepts. Planning of this magnitude would certainly stifle future problems, isolate the existing contracts that were faltering, and create additional need of attention. Lacking in this strategic planning, as evidenced by the role of a continuation of borrowing and expansion, was a philosophy of maintaining or retrenching.

The Securities and Exchange Commission studied this phenomenon and elected to review a study, thereby accepting the proposal of a new organizational structure called a combination real estate investment trust that was authored by the author of this book.

The author, being highly cognizant of the inherent fallacies within the equity trusts and debt/mortgage trusts, the only types of real estate investment trusts then approved, chose the middle ground as representative of the best investment policies of the formerly described trusts.

This basic concept was expanded in philosophy policies based upon percentages of investment capital. This policy should fundamentally remove the pressure of a healthy real estate investment trust to remain viable.

The over-balanced trust, wherein the majority of funds are placed only in equity investments, which do not necessarily meet the ideal criteria, creates a faulty portfolio. The other trust style of debt/mortgage trusts falters in a like manner, placing mortgages on projects that are not necessarily projecting themselves as future star performers.

The author introduced an investment style of control that had not been in existence previously, that of allocation of funds per type of projects. This direction allows for a spread of risks that is understandably desired in trusts.

The real estate investment trusts were not a highly studied group, as evidenced by the lack of data in the library systems. Brokerage firms analyzed them from two points of view: (1) the price and (2) the earnings. This method, hardly beneficial to this research study, did, indeed, accomplish the goals of the brokerage house and customers/investors.

Comparative analysis was not an organized program or requirement associated with any agency's responsibilities.

The comparison made by the brokerage firms resulted in price/earnings ratios—the higher the earnings compared to the price, the higher the degree of attentiveness relative to the churning of available stock sales. The indications of this technique were representative of switching buyers and sellers, individual as well as institutional investor capital.

The importance of philosophical determinations, both internally and externally, tends to flex the organization's concepts, precepts, and current and future programs. This flexing then molds the current and future events, decisions, and policies then based upon those areas that were perceived within the scope of those philosophical decisions.

The monetary market, the contraction or expansion of the economy, growth demands, economic demands, current and future demands, past performances, and historical documentation of contracts are but a few of the determinations that should be in constant review. This list of determinations can include five hundred or more in a single contract negotiation and a lesser degree in others. The determinations eventually evolve toward finalizing management goals.

Trustees—the senior authorities—of real estate investment trusts are charged with the responsibility of investing funds responsibly, logically, and prudently. This responsibility should be considered in their staking of their trustee position and management's future and reputation. All fall within the area of moral philosophies. Abdication of those responsibilities to less senior management most certainly quickens failures of the trust organizations.

4
Findings and Results

Thorough research, modification, and methods will be incorporated to present the more contemporary approach of real estate investment trust management.

Having uncovered oblique and parallax views, the author will provide proof that the events of the 1970s indicate the necessity for the solidification of methods, concepts, and philosophies that were in definite need of modification and major changes.

As previously stated, the comparative method was by choice and the best method for the analysis of each trust. By comparing the stated philosophies and physical restraints—the abstract and the reality—of each trust subsequent to the actual data of the financial statement, the author determined that a percentage of stated philosophies and physical restraints were not as originally stated or perceived. Trust statistics indicate an accomplishment of an average of 70 percent of their stated goals as the break-even point toward the actual accomplishments versus the stated philosophies.

Utilizing the 70 percent ratios for both the debt/mortgage trusts and the equity trusts, a determination can be made as to whether the trusts are, in actuality, a debt/mortgage trust or an equity trust, or, in a few cases, a balanced trust by accumulating a fifty-fifty percentage of both equity assets and debt/mortgage assets. This, theoretically, should add stability and credibility to their trust's portfolio performance.

Research of the stated philosophies versus the balance sheets, a summary of which is provided on the previous lists in chapter 2, reveals that 95 are debt/mortgage trusts, 62 are equity trusts and 7 are balanced investment trusts, totaling 164 as viable trusts and members of the trust association.

The real estate investment trust industry grew from total obscurity, developing into a giant of an industry in a ten-year period (1961–71), most of which developed in the stated three-year period (1969–1971). All 164 businesses started from a zero organization structure, spiraling toward mammoth organizational structures. The total employment buildup, including staff and management, equaled a count of 28,700, the majority arriving on the unfolding scene from 1969 through the year 1973. Discounting those in the older trusts that had developed prior to 1969, the number totaled 22,088 new employees.

These personnel were of the highest caliber in quality and training one could acquire toward literacy regarding investment knowledge. These employees were either in body on location of the trusts or contracted to provide a service under other institutions' directions.

Utilizing the five-year (sixty-month) span analysis, it should follow that extremes or excesses would appear in numerous areas, particularly in that area concerning the efficiency of the newly hired staff.

The employment frequency and training necessities are two of the major concerns that indicate the physical restraints of newly employed personnel within each department of each trust. Regardless of how highly and well-motivated they may be, training is necessary for both the literate and illiterate in trust management and support operations.

Using the predetermined number of new employees (22,088), thereby staffing the numerous positions through the years 1969–73, a five-year buildout should indicate the training cycle of each employee; ascertaining the micro–employee-training and the macro–employee-training in time should also offer a perspective of responsibility of management and trustees of investor funds. From this new perspective, it should offer a view in the determination of experience versus philosophies of management in growth toward the expansion of monetary explosion and training/expansion of numbers of employees.

Initially, using the macro approach to total employees for the five-year (sixty-month) period inclusive of the years 1969 through 1973, there were 28,700 employees, staff and management, under contract or in-house under supervision, all newly hired or transferred into this phase from older trust organizations. All were trained internally. No schools were active to train employees as specialists in trusts. A percentage of the employees were terminated, some left under their own volition, and a few were rehired and retrained.

Utilizing a linear graph approach, charting the requirements of training necessities, in which new employee growth problematically increased uniformly over the total span of five years, plus or minus a few percentage points, this minor deviation is not considered major in this analysis.

Based upon this linear expansion theory, an average of 478 new employees joined the ranks of the trusts each month, integrating within each of the 164 trusts for the total sixty-month period. This staffing was undoubtedly greater in 1973, with a smaller quantity in the previous years of 1972, 1971, 1970, and 1969.

Recalling that trusts came into being in 1961, a few trusts staffed previous employees with continuous training in all viable operations. Deducting those former employees (6,612) and ending the balances of their financial growth in 1968 (net assets equaling $4,000,220,000), calculations can approximate with sufficient reliability the status of each trust based upon the amount of dollars each trust was managing versus the number of employees in each trust.

Tabulating the assets of each trust through the year 1973, the volume of dollars in assets totalled $17,366,130,000. This is cumulative for all types of trusts.

Macro tabulating the three styles of trusts of managed assets: debt/mortgage trusts totaled $13,274,470,000, the equity trusts $3,499,530,000, and the balanced trusts $592,300,000.

Again using the expansion of uniformity through the sixty-month period, the theoretical and problematic decrease of employees was a 20 percent reduction of the average number of 478 employees in the year 1972 and a reduction of 20 percent in each year through 1969. This number should be adjusted to ascertain the beginning employee count starting in the year 1969. Using the employee count of 28,700 as of the end of year 1973 and dividing that number into the dollar figure of the ending balance of each trust, a summarization of the numbers should indicate the numerical status of personnel in each trust in each year and include the monetary expansion threshold of each trust mode.

Using the total dollars within the trust averages in 1969 and dividing by the dollar volume for which each employee was theoretically responsible, an employee count of 6,612 were on staff in 1969. New employees hired during the sixty-month period equaled 22,088; 368 new employees were entering the new field of real estate investment trusts each month, an average of 2.9 (say 3) new hirees each month. This average is developed by the sum of fractional ratios based upon the variable growth rates in expansion of capital of each of the 164 trusts.

Theoretical approaches as previously described are meaningful to determine certain degrees of function; however, management in business makes the decisions in the overall majority of all types of organizations. The real estate investment trusts management was the decision-making body. That grouping of trustees and upper echelon of each organization can be classified in the 10 percent range of total staff personnel.

That percentage number of decision makers being the responsible group, it appears that in 1968 the group of decision makers numbered 661 and grew in numbers to 2,870 aggressive, business-indoctrinated, well-educated people, seasoned in financial investment programs. A growth of new decision makers of 2,209 meant an average of 36 new employees each month or a 1.6 percent increase each month, corresponding to the overall number of new employees acting as support personnel of 2.1 percent each month.

This is well within the parameters of an expanding business organizational theme. Using the linear scale, as previously outlined, we can view the triad of organizations—personnel staffing, decision-maker percentages and volume of transactions—to monitor each organization.

Debt/mortgage real estate investment trusts with a balance sheet totaling $13,274,470,000 would share in the largest percentage of employees. Using $604,917 responsibility of management per employee, a total of all trust employees is indicated as 21,944.

Equity real estate investment trust balance sheets showing a sum total of $3,499,530,000 would employ 5,785.

Balanced real estate investment trust balance sheets indicating a sum total of $592,300,000 would employ 979.

Decision-making personnel in the debt/mortgage trusts total 2,194, in the equity trusts 578, and in the balanced funds 98, all sophisticated in business acumen.

The average transaction of most real estate investment trusts approximated $2 million. By dividing the average transaction number into the gross assets, the number of transactions that need vigilance should indicate the service activity necessary to fulfill the task.

Debt/mortgage real estate investment trusts had 6,637,235,000 transactions, equity real estate investment trusts 1,749,765,000 transactions, and balanced real estate investment trusts 296,150,000 transactions, or a sum total of 8,683,150,000 transactions spread over a sixty-month period of business activity.

Using 28,700 as the total employees in all trusts, it is indicated that each employee was to maintain vigilance over 302,548 transactions. Then using a 365-day year, the number of transactions each day that each employee would necessarily review was 828. Using an eight-hour shift per day causes one to be perplexed, as this indicates the number of 103 per hour, every day of each year—better yet, one every fifty-eight seconds of every minute, of every hour, of every day, of every week, fifty-two weeks a year. The advent of computers certainly was a necessity to comprehend this style of vigilance.

As spectacular as it may seem, based upon the time spent on the training of employees—as offered by management—supervisors spend no more than 1½ hours per day in training. United Research Company, in the December 1987 issue of the *Wall Street Journal* stated: "Supervisors spend barely 1½ hours a day actually supervising subordinates." Following this same line of thought, Robert Half International, the leading employment executive search and placement firm, was quoted from research they had completed by surveying the personnel chiefs of a majority of companies: "Top executives are better in reading, writing and arithmetic than middle managers. And middle managers get better marks than their staffers. They're all weak in writing and spelling."

Advisory organizations were experiencing great difficulty throughout their hiring, training, and management career program. Advisory groups were groping to locate projects—good projects—that the various real estate investment trusts desired and for which they allocated their respective investments.

One may ask: How did these new organizations obtain funds of such magnitude in such a short period of time? Reviewing the prior sections, real estate investment trusts are formed to provide a service to a specific arena of the public, namely real estate; investment opportunities range from mortgages, developing, owning, and venturing, all through some form of contractual obligation.

Start-up capitalization of these 164 real estate investment trusts is acquired through an investment of dollars, generally funded by the same organization that forms the trust corpus. Desirable projects are ferreted out, and funding of these projects is then through the debt/mortgage, equity, or balanced trust methodologies. This nucleus of events and desires develops into an income and benefit program, interesting to investors. The purpose, when the program manifests, is to infill their investment portfolios.

Shares of certificates of beneficial interest are available through numerous avenues; all shares sold are to meet investors' demands.

Additional leveraging of capitalization of trusts is through borrowing from institutional investors. The instruments used in the borrowing of funds are notes, debentures, mortgages, commercial paper, credit lines, and certificates of deposit, just to name a few.

Mushrooming of growth assets and generally more liabilities occur until restraints are initiated by management, restricting growth in most areas. Growth then recedes as operations of the trusts attain a satisfaction of success, and management then displays a style of containment, conservation, and opting for the quality opportunities.

The areas of the country in which real estate investment trusts developed were overwhelmingly located on the East Coast and, second, in the southeastern portion of the country. Investments tended to remain in the general area.

Representatives such as advisory groups, certified public accountants, attorneys, and other contractor firms varied from local to major national organizations.

The pay scale of contracted labor was so varied that if one chose, he would have the opportunity to have 164 choices or variations of each to develop the contracted labor schedules for future organization formation.

Philosophies of management were critically diverse for each of the 164 real estate investment trusts. A combination, theoretically to ensure success of policies, procedures, and restraints is found among all 164, tailored to each organization's trustees' personalities.

Real estate investment represents the major form of wealth not only in the United States, but perhaps internationally. The attention of specialized management directing real estate investment trusts is charged with the responsibility of applying the absolutes of investment principles and techniques with materials that set the tone for the institution's settings. The results of this responsible action have major impact on the nation's economy and directly or indirectly affect the lives and fortunes of all of us.

Probably the greatest social cost of all this shuffling of funds lay not in the peculiar profit that any of the special interests won for management but in the fact that their interplay— undisciplined by any strong policy leadership generated through a learning process—added to the misdirection of efforts that subjected the investors to the costs of an inefficient system of investments. Thus management lacked tradition or experience in the administrative skills or organization, which more ambitious investment management required.

Real estate is a dynamic field for the most astute; changes occur without precedent and occur quickly. This is especially true with regard to mortgages and mortgage constraints. This is the area of management acumen that requires judicial surveillance—not passive—as indicated in the downward spiral of failures caused by this major element of fundamental precepts.

The attractiveness of certain types of property as priority investment media follows a pattern of change, not only in types but in areas of investment and locale and through population migration.

Operational expenses of a property float—generally higher—and investment projections within the budget guidelines as ad valorem taxes, utilities, maintenance, labor, and management are subject to constant review and updating.

A good product is a basic essential for a successful investment. The necessity to look beyond the facts and figures of the proposal of the project is paramount in the management decision-making process to determine at the inception if it is satisfactory in logistics and soundness wherever the market demand for space, services, and amenities are offered.

Investments in real estate are not made in a static economy or environment. Influences of social, physical, economic, and local and national political factors are constantly working, creating a climate of change.

An awareness of the speed, direction, strength, and duration of trends, if at all determinable, must be dealt with by a well- organized planning staff.

Real estate and real estate markets are heavily influenced by local, county, state, and federal governments at all levels. This area of study requires the micro-analyzation on which many statistical data are published. The local representatives may offer the first source of data in their growth planning departments. The other agencies plan through the next twenty years in most cases. The data is available; it requires time to sort it out, this being management's area of responsibility.

The Securities and Exchange Commission controls the market when developing investments in securities; however, in real estate there is not a centrally controlled or organized market. Local markets predominate the real estate industry.

Planning commissions are coming to the forefront to control developments specifically toward the area of master planning.

The supply of properties is seldom in balance with demand. Supplies cannot be adjusted quickly. This is one of the fundamental reasons that the building industry attempts to build as closely as possible to the demand; however, this too is questionable when a number of contractors are vying for the same market.

Financing arrangements are expensive and complex. Real estate developments are for a long term and inflexible, creating a lifelong asset. Once the decision is made, one must get on with the development; the financing is much safer when the project is complete and in use.

High dollar value is the basic reasoning bringing forth the market for investment of real estate investment trusts. The acceptance of the responsibility of bringing the buyers and sellers of the product together is a characteristic not to be forgotten. Satellite developments can be as profitable with less competition as crowding the overbuilt areas with hopeful appeal.

Individual differences of each project limit comparison with similarities to other accomplishments of projects gone before. Marketing skills are paramount in ascertaining the actual needs versus the theoretical desires of the builders, borrowers or equity owners. Tying this data with overall planning assists in a valuable management decision process.

The market must be there to bring about the intended results of the investment purpose. Buildings are in place and, it is hoped, in use for one-hundred-year spans. Intelligent decisions of great magnitude foreshadow premium investment practices, and investment capital should flow only to those long-term needs of society.

5
Summary

The combination real estate investment trusts set forth in Appendix B are totally inclusive of those modifications as suggested by the author throughout this book.

Appendix B will prove to many a boon of wealth, knowledge, and time-honored information. These documents represent the first of many trust originations but one who publishes their proprietary documents.

It is with joy that I share these documents to assist those entrepreneurs in real estate investment trust developments.

Appendixes

Appendix A

CHART 1

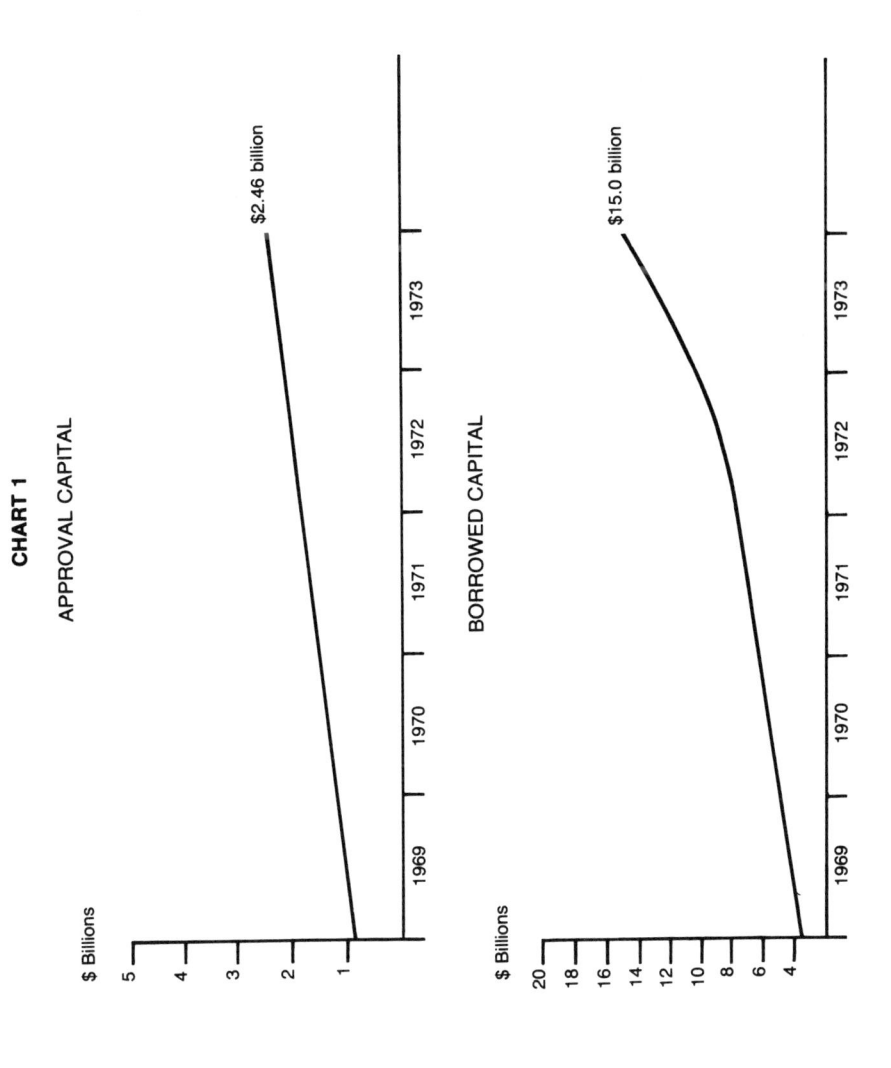

APPROVAL CAPITAL

$ Billions

$2.46 billion

1969 1970 1971 1972 1973

BORROWED CAPITAL

$ Billions

$15.0 billion

1969 1970 1971 1972 1973

CHART 2

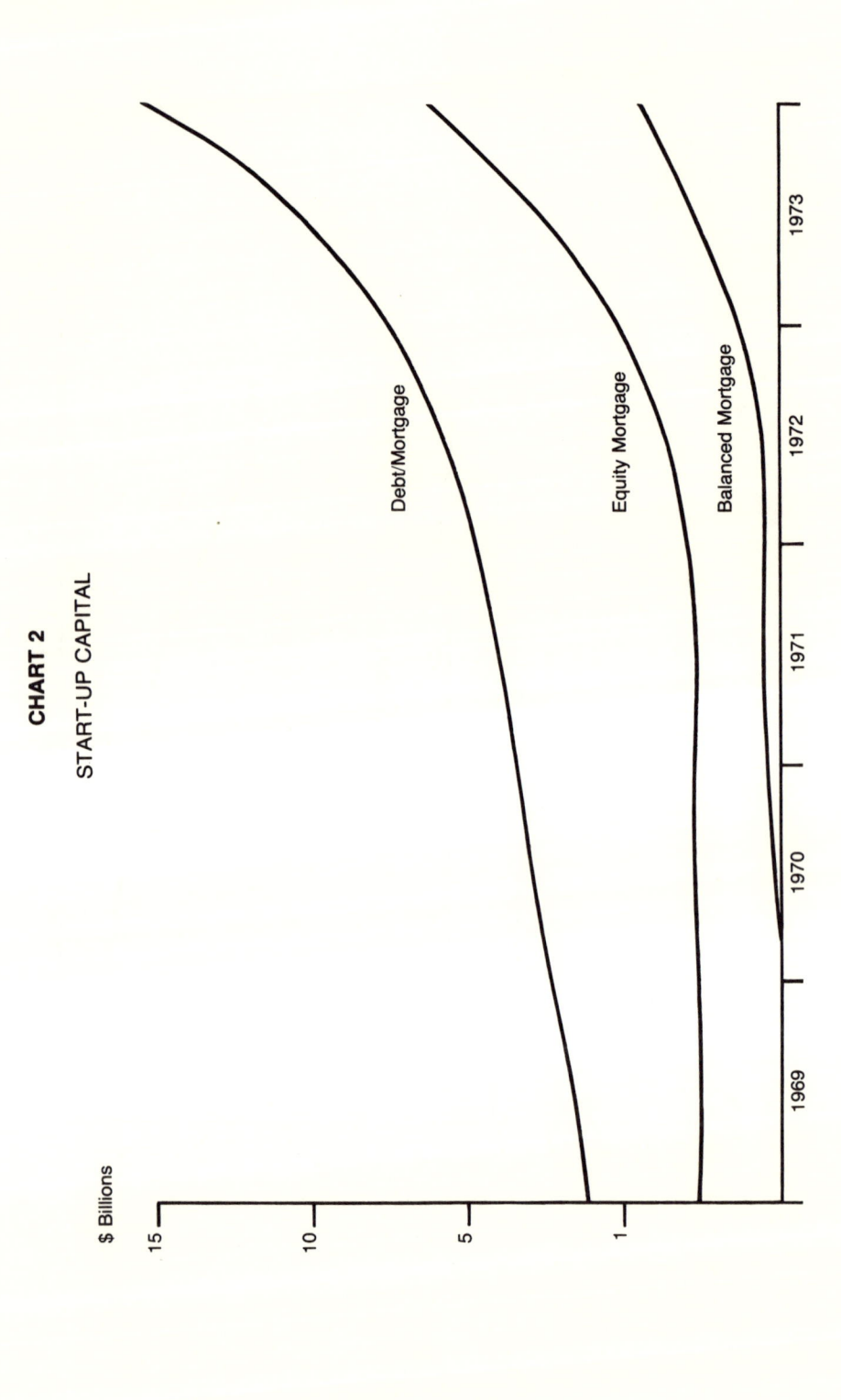

START-UP CAPITAL

CHART 3

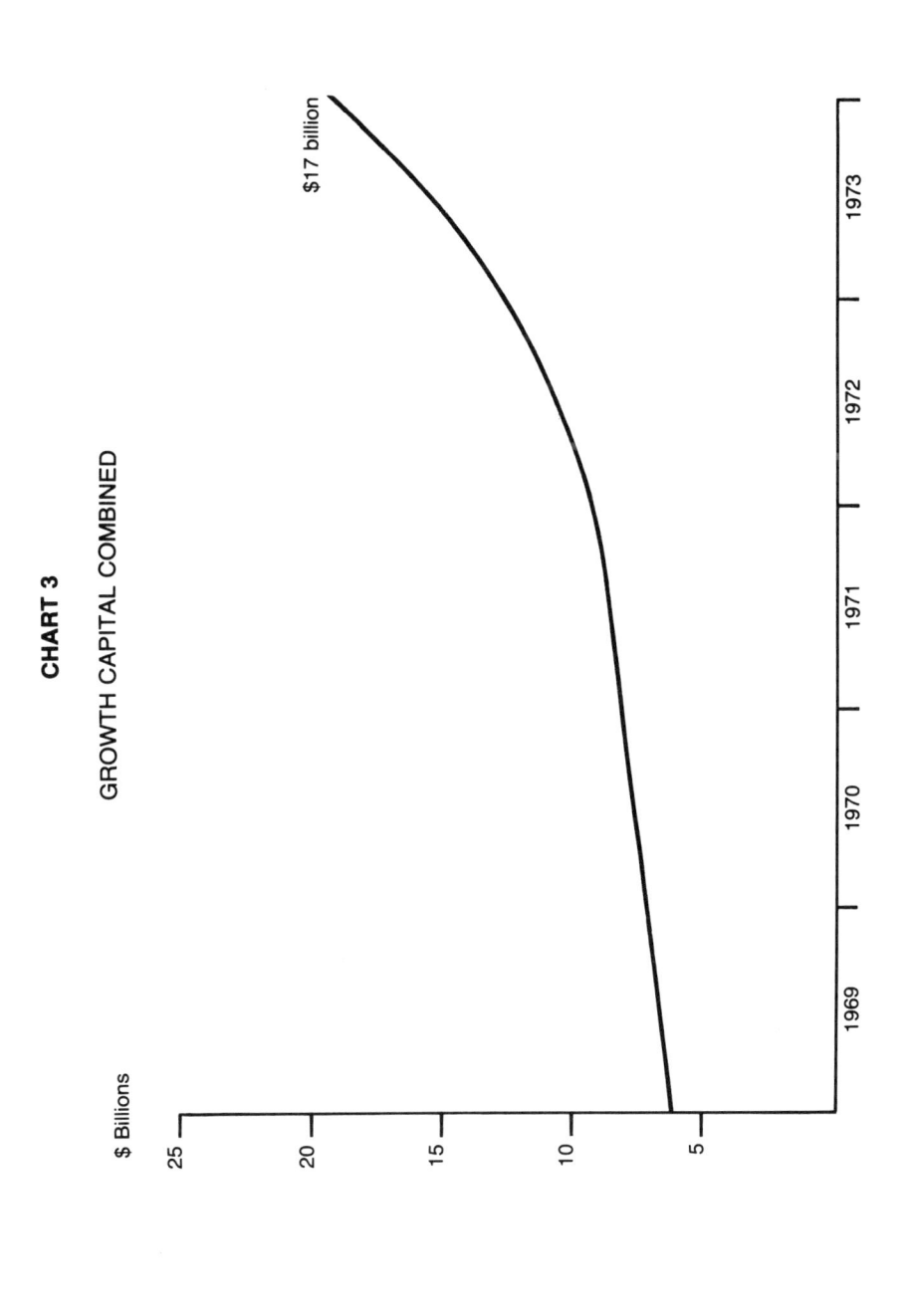

GROWTH CAPITAL COMBINED

$ Billions

$17 billion

25
20
15
10
5

1969   1970   1971   1972   1973

CHART 4

RISE/PEAK/FALL/RISE
VIABLE REITS

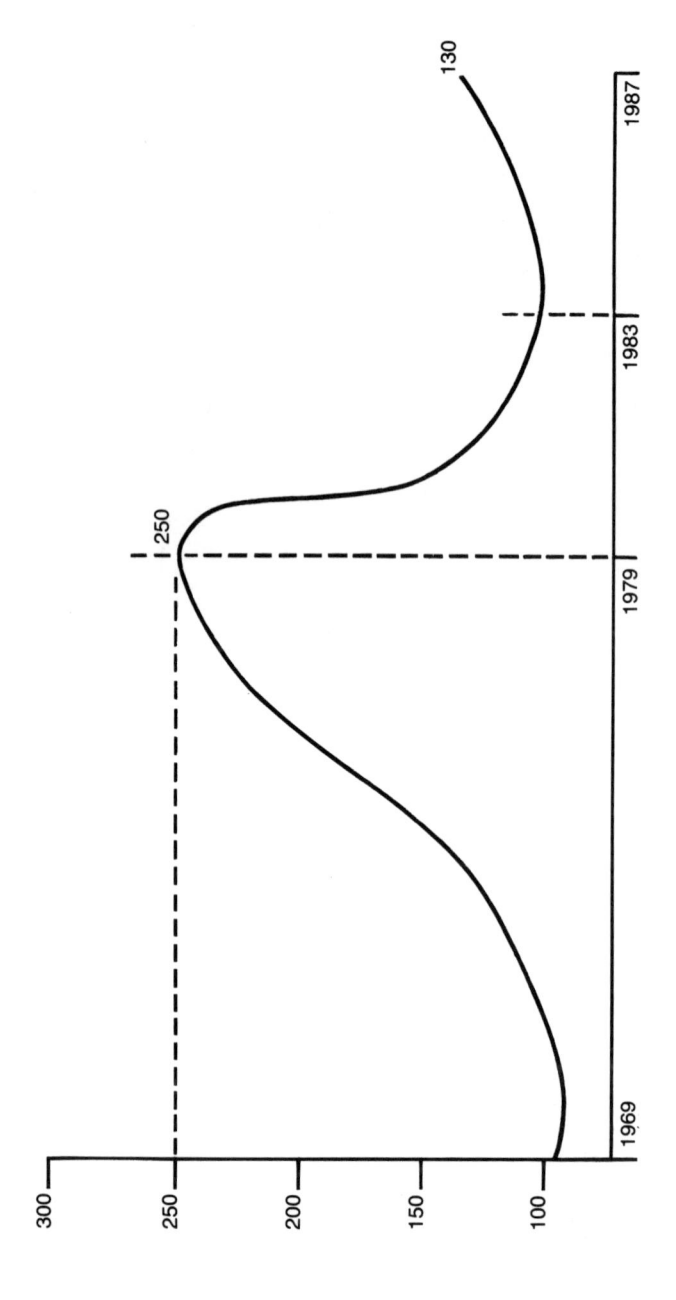

CHART 5

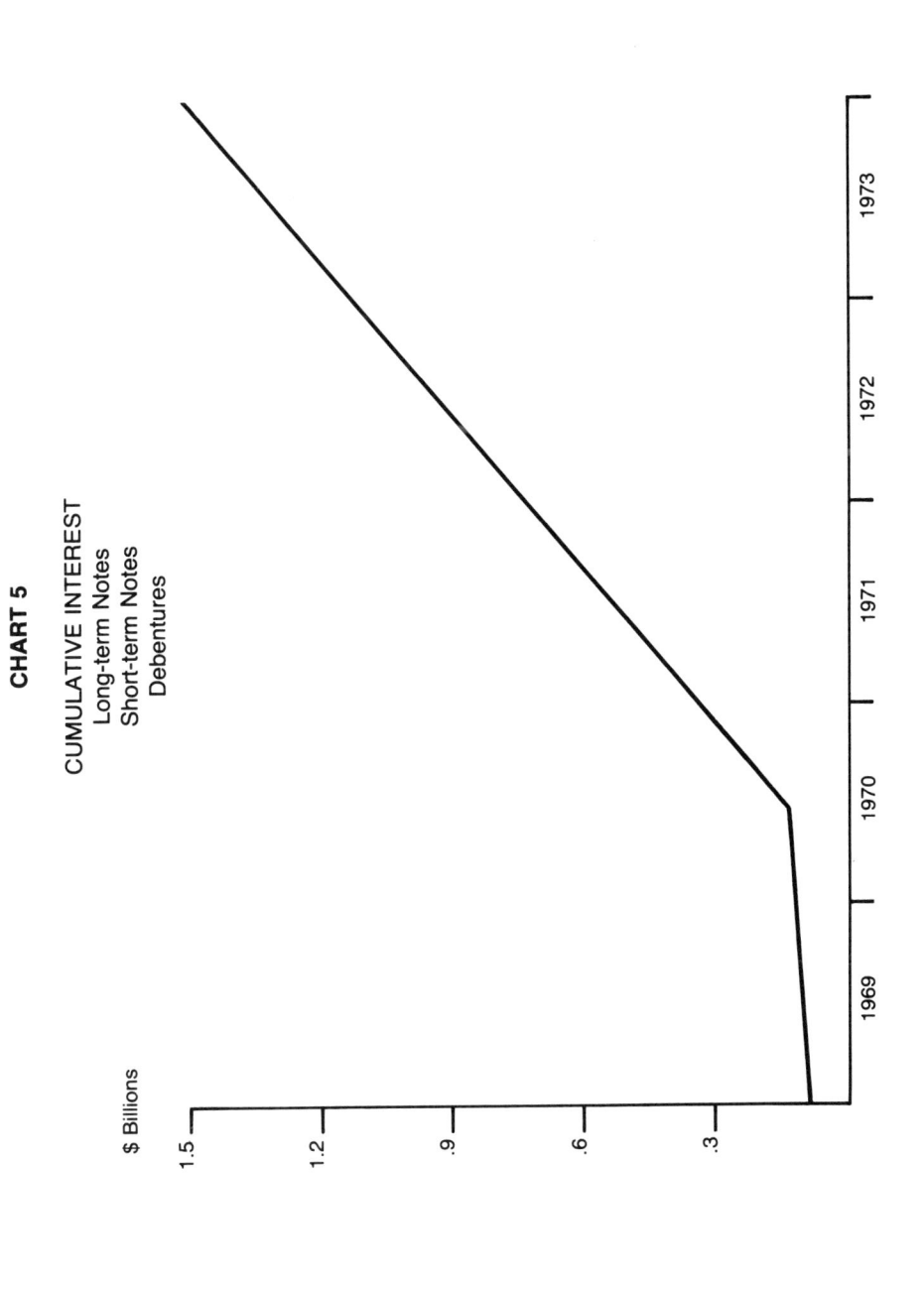

CUMULATIVE INTEREST
Long-term Notes
Short-term Notes
Debentures

$ Billions

1.5
1.2
.9
.6
.3

1969   1970   1971   1972   1973

Appendix B

AS FILED WITH THE SECURITIES AND EXCHANGE
COMMISSION
REGISTRATION NO. 1

SECURITIES AND EXCHANGE COMMISSION
WASHINGTON, D.C. 20549

FORM S-11
REGISTRATION STATEMENT
UNDER
THE SECURITIES ACT OF 1933

FIRST NATIONAL REALTY TRUST
[exact name of registrant as specified in governing instrument]

[address of principal executive office]

	Copies to:
ABC	Mr. XYZ
First National Realty Trust	Attorney at Law
	[Address]
[name and address of agent or service]	

Approximate date of commencement of proposed sale to the public:
As soon as practicable after the effective date of
this Registration Statement

CALCULATION OF REGISTRATION FEE

Title of Securities Being Registered	Amount Registered	Proposed Offering Price Per Unit	Proposed Maximum Aggregate Offering Price	Amount of Registration Fee
Shares of Beneficial Interest	5,000,000	$10.00	$50,000,000	$15,000.00

PROSPECTUS

FIRST NATIONAL REALTY TRUST
5,000,000 Shares of Beneficial Interest

($1.00 Par Value)

Prior to this offering, there has been no market for the Shares of Beneficial Interest (the "Shares") of the Trust. Accordingly, the public offering price has been determined arbitrarily by the Trust.

THESE SECURITIES ARE SUBJECT TO CERTAIN RISK FACTORS
SEE "RISK FACTORS"

THESE SECURITIES HAVE NOT BEEN APPROVED OR DISAPPROVED BY THE SECURITIES AND EXCHANGE COMMISSION NOR HAS THE COMMISSION PASSED UPON THE ACCURACY OR ADEQUACY OF THIS PROSPECTUS. ANY REPRESENTATION TO THE CONTRARY IS A CRIMINAL OFFENSE.

THE ATTORNEY GENERAL OF THE STATE OF NEW YORK HAS NOT PASSED ON OR ENDORSED THE MERITS OF THIS OFFERING. ANY REPRESENTATION TO THE CONTRARY IS UNLAWFUL.

	Public Offering Price	Selling Commissions (2)	Proceeds to the Trust (1)
Per Share (3) ...	$ 10.00	$0.85	$9.15
Total Minimum ...	$ 1,000,000	$85,000	$915,000
Total Maximum ...	$50,000,000	$4,250,000	$45,750,000

The Shares are being offered through selected members of the Stock Exchanges & Underwriters on a "best efforts" basis, when, as and if issued by the Trust and subject to prior sale.

(1) Before deducting organizational and other expenses payable by the Trust in connection with this offering estimated to aggregate $200,000. (See "Use of Proceeds") In the event only the minimum number of Shares are sold (which is only 1/15 of the total offering), this will be $2.00 per Share. However, the Advisor, First National Advisors, Inc., has agreed that in the event selling commissions and other expenses of the offering exceed 15 percent of the gross proceeds of the offering such expenses will be paid by First National Advisors, Inc., and not by the Trust. The proceeds of this offering will be escrowed until a minimum of 100,000 Shares are sold. In the event 100,000 Shares are not sold within six months after the date of this Prospectus, all proceeds will be returned to the investors and the costs of the offering will be borne by the Trust, which has previously sold 20,000 Shares to the sponsors. This offering will terminate twelve months after the date of this Prospectus.
(2) First National Realty Trust will pay sales commissions to participating members of the Stock Exchange Members & Underwriters at the rate of 0.85 percent of the subscription price of the Shares sold to purchasers obtained by them. Any underwriter who effects sales for the Trust and any other person who participates in the distribution of the Shares may be deemed to be an "underwriter" as that term is defined in the Securities Act of 1933. The Trust has agreed to indemnify soliciting underwriters against certain civil liabilities, including liabilities under the Securities Act of 1933. (See "Plan of Distribution")
(3) The minimum initial purchase will be Five Hundred ($500.00) Dollars (50 Shares).

Summary

Trust: First National Realty Trust

Offering: Minimum $1,000,000; Maximum $50,000,000

Trustees: See "Management of the Trust"

Management: See "The Advisor"

Trust Objectives:

   (1) To invest in short-term construction and development loans.
   (2) To acquire equities in real property, most of which may be acquired in exchange for Trust Shares.
   (3) To invest in medium- and long-term mortgage loans.

   No assurance can be given that these primary objectives will be reached. For a description of other objectives see "Investment and Operating Policies of the Trust."

Dividend Policy: The Trust intends initially to make quarterly distributions of 90 percent of net taxable income. (See "Distributions")

Trust Borrowing: The Trust intends to borrow additional capital, but has no commitments at this time. (See "Borrowing Policy")

Trustees Fees: See "Management of the Trust."

Advisor Fees: See "Compensation Payable by the Trust to the Advisor" and "The Advisor—Compensation Provisions."

The Trust

First National Realty Trust (the "Trust") has been established to invest in a diversified portfolio of real property investments. Initially the Trust will invest in short-term construction and development loans. (See "Use of Proceeds" and "Initial Investments") As the initial short-term loans mature, the Trust intends to maintain a substantial investment in similar short-term loans and may diversify the Trust's portfolio to include equity interests in real estate. The Trust may at any time acquire equity interests in exchange for Shares of the Trust. The Trust will invest in medium- and long-term mortgage loans. (See "Investment and Operating Policies of the Trust")

Responsibility for management of the Trust is vested exclusively in the Trustees. (See "Management of the Trust") In addition, the Trust has entered into a contract with First National Advisors, Inc. (see "Advisor"), pursuant to which the Advisor has undertaken to seek out and present to the Trustees investment opportunities and to provide investment and financial advice. (See "The Advisor")

The Trust intends to qualify as a real estate investment trust under Sections 856-858 of the Internal Revenue Code. Under those sections, if certain conditions are met, the Trust will not be taxed on that portion of its taxable income which is distributed to shareholders, if at least 90 percent of its real estate investment trust taxable income is distributed. (See "Taxation")

The Trust is a business trust organized under the laws of the State of California, pursuant to a Declaration of Trust dated August, 1983. The offices of the Trust and the Advisor are:

Compensation Payable by the Trust to the Advisor

The following summary shows the compensation that may be paid by the Trust to the Advisor and its affiliates. This summary is qualified by the information presented in the section of this Prospectus entitled "The Advisor—Compensation Provisions" and "Risk Factors—Fixed Expenses." For a description of compensation payable to unaffiliated Trustees, see "Management of the Trust."

To Whom Paid	Type of Compensation	Amounts to Be Paid
Advisor	Advisory Fees	Regular compensation at the rate of 4/50 of 1.00 percent per month (96/100 of 1.00 percent per annum) of book value of Invested Assets (including closed but undisbursed loan commitments). In addition, incentive compensation equal to 10 percent of the net capital gain plus extraordinary nonrecurring items of income of the Trust for the fiscal year, plus 10 percent of the amount, if any, by which net profits for such fiscal year exceed 10 percent per annum of the average net worth of the Trust during such year.
Stock Exchange Members & Underwriters	Sales Commission	A sales commission of 0.85 percent of the sale price of Shares sold by it.

If operating expenses of the Trust exceed certain limits, the Advisor is required to bear these expenses up to the amount of the Advisory Fees otherwise payable. (See "The Advisor—Compensation Provisions") In any given fiscal year, the Advisor or its affiliates may receive from parties other than the Trust a real estate brokerage commission in connection with the purchase of Trust assets (no such commission being payable by the Trust to the Advisor in that fiscal year shall be reduced by an amount equal to the amount of such commission received by the Advisor or its affiliates from third parties, but not exceeding an amount equal to 100 percent of compensation otherwise payable in that fiscal year to the Advisor of the Trust. (See "The Advisor—Compensation Provisions")

Risk Factors

Risk on Default on Loans

All real property investments are subject to some degree of risk. The mortgage loans in which the Trust intends to invest may be insured or guaranteed. However, in the event of a default by a borrower, it may be necessary for the Trust to foreclose its mortgage or engage in negotiations which may involve further outlays to protect the Trust's investment. The mortgage securing the Trust's loans may be or become, in certain cases, subordinated to mechanic's liens, materialmen's liens or government liens and, in those instances in which the Trust invests in junior mortgages, to liens of senior mortgages. In such cases it may become necessary, in order to protect a particular investment, for the Trust to make payments on underlying senior or prior liens in order to maintain the current status of a prior lien or to discharge it entirely. It is possible that the total amount recovered by the Trust in such cases may be less than its total investment, resulting in losses to the Trust.

Some of the Trust's mortgage loans may provide for payments of principal on an amortization basis longer than the term of the loan. Such loans would require a substantial portion of the principal thereof to be paid upon maturity and, therefore, may be subject to greater risk of default and default in a greater magnitude than loans providing for equal amortization of principal and interest over their terms.

The Declaration of Trust authorizes the Trust to make lease-hold mortgage loans and junior mortgage loans, which involve additional risk, such as possible defaults by tenants or defaults under prior mortgages.

Short-Term Investment Risks

Short-term construction and development loans secured by mortgages are subject to substantial risk because the ability of the borrower to complete the project and repay the loan may be affected by a number of factors, including: adverse changes in interest rates or the availability of long-term mortgage funds; local conditions such as excessive building resulting in an excess supply of space, or a decrease in employment reducing economic conditions; and the ability of the borrowing builder or developer to control costs and to conform to plans, specifications and time schedules, which will depend upon his management and financial capabilities and which may also be affected by strikes, adverse weather, the "energy crisis" and other conditions beyond his control. Such contingencies and adverse factors can deplete the borrower's funds and working capital and could result in substantial deficiencies precluding compliance with the conditions of commitments for long-term mortgages relied on as a primary source for repayment of such loans. Also, the Trust may make short-term mortgage construction loans without commitments for long-term financing or standby commitments or may itself issue such commitments. Development loans are ordinarily made without requiring a commitment for construction or permanent mortgage financing and are, therefore, subject to additional risks.

Long-Term Investment Risks

Long-term mortgage loans and equity real estate investments may tend to limit the ability of the Trust to vary its portfolio promptly in response to changing economic, financial and investment conditions. Such investments may be subject to risks such as adverse changes in general economic conditions and local conditions such as excessive building, resulting in an oversupply of existing space, or decreases in employment, reducing the demand for real estate in the area, as well as other factors affecting real estate values including the attractiveness of the properties to tenants, neighborhood values, and the credit and financial stability of the lessees of properties in which the Trust has investments.

In some instances, the Trust may make a construction loan and a long-term loan on the same property. In such cases, the Trust's investment in that property may be subject to both short-term investment risks and the long-term investment risks indicated above.

Equity Investment Risks

Real estate equity investments which the Trust may make will generally be subject to the lien of a mortgage loan or loans, which may represent the major portion of the value of the property. Payments on such mortgages may at times be in excess of income generated by the properties. If the mortgage payments are not met, the Trust may sustain a loss on its equity investment as a result of foreclosure of the property. In addition, such mortgage payments, as well as certain other expenditures associated with equity investments (principally real estate taxes, maintenance and management costs), are not necessarily decreased by events adversely affecting the Trust's income from such investments. The Trust may also purchase equity investments under conditional sales contracts, involving similar risks. Equity investments are also subject to such risks as adverse changes in interest rates, lack of available long-term mortgage funds, and the inability of the Trust to provide adequate maintenance of its properties. Any investment affected by such events could become a burden on the Trust's other assets, impairing or precluding distributions to shareholders.

In land purchase-leaseback transactions, the Trust may purchase land underlying existing or proposed improvements. Both the land owned by the Trust and the improvements thereon may be subject to the lien of a first mortgage which has priority over the Trust's interest in the land. In some instances the ground lessee may have the right to refinance the first mortgage one or more times with continuing priority. A default by a ground lessee or other premature termination of the lease may result in the Trust's being unable to recover its investment unless the property is sold or released on favorable terms. The value of the land and improvements may depend, in large part, on the credit and financial stability of the tenants in occupancy.

High Investment-to-Value Ratio

Because of the flexible investment policies of the Trust, the investments of the Trust may be made through a variety of financing techniques such as land purchase-leaseback transactions and net lease financings, some of which may involve investment-to-value ratios up to 100 percent. To the extent that the Trust might have to rely on the security for such financings in the event of default by the borrower, the risk of loss to the Trust will be increased.

Trust Loan Commitments

The Trust's commitments to make investments may exceed its available cash. Also the Trust's cash flow is dependent in part on the ability of the borrowers to repay their loans. Thus, in order to meet its commitments the Trust may be required to liquidate certain of its investments on unfavorable terms.

Leveraging

Depending on the availability and cost of borrowing, the Trust intends to use leverage (borrowing funds to increase its assets available for investments). Such leveraging will be effected through long-term debt, commercial paper and bank lines of credit. (See "Borrowing Policy") The resulting higher level of obligations may increase the Trust's exposure to risk of loss. In order to repay such borrowings, the Trust may be required to liquidate certain of its investments, which may have an adverse effect on its operations. Further, in the event the effective yield to the Trust with respect to its investments should prove to be less than the cost of borrowed funds to the Trust, operating results of the Trust would be adversely affected. Under the terms of the Advisory Agreement, the Advisor's compensation is based, in part, on average book value of Invested Assets, and the investment of such borrowed funds may increase the compensation payable to the Advisor. The Trust has no commitments for additional funds and no assurance can be given that any will be available. (See "The Advisor—Compensation Provisions")

Competition

The Trust will be competing against commercial banks, savings and loan associations, mortgage bankers and other lenders, including other real estate investment trusts for the placement of construction and development loans. In the field of long-term mortgage financing, the Trust will be competing against life insurance companies, mutual savings banks, mortgage bankers, savings and loan associations, pension funds, the Federal National Mortgage Association and other lenders, including other real estate investment trusts. In other areas of investment permitted to the Trust there is also a wide variety of competing lenders and investors. The Trust will be funded with not less than $1,050,000 nor more than $45,750,000. Consequently, many of its competitors have greater financial resources than the Trust. An increase in the availability of investment funds may increase competition for suitable investment opportunities, resulting in reduced yields. If the Trust commences operations with minimum proceeds, any single investment error will affect the Trust more than if it had a larger sum of money invested.

Fixed Expenses

Interest and required amortization payments on outstanding debt and operating expenses of the Trust (including certain compensation of the Advisor) must be met without regard to the Trust's profitability. (See "The Advisor—Compensation Provision")

Possible Dilution

The Trust is authorized, without approval of the shareholders, to issue additional Shares, warrants, and debt securities convertible into Shares for cash or property. Such transactions may dilute the interests of the shareholders in the Trust's income and assets and may dilute the interests which may be obtained by the holders of the warrants.

Shareholder Liability

The Declaration of Trust provides that no shareholder shall be subject to any personal liability for the acts or obligations of the Trust and that every written undertaking made by the Trust shall contain a provision that the undertaking is not binding upon any of the shareholders personally. No personal liability will attach to the shareholders for contract claims under any instrument containing such provisions except possibly in a few jurisdictions where the shareholders may be held personally liable. However, the Declaration of Trust provides that upon payment of any such liability the shareholders will be entitled to reimbursements from the general assets of the Trust. The Trustees intend to carry insurance which they consider adequate to cover any foreseeable tort liability, to the extent such insurance is available at reasonable rates.

Interest Ceilings under Usury Statutes

Loans made by the Trust ordinarily will be subject to statutory restrictions limiting the maximum interest charges and imposing penalties which may include restitution of excess interest and, in some cases, may affect enforceability of the debt. There can be no assurance that all or a portion of the charges and fees which the Trust receives on its loans may not be held to exceed the statutory maximums, in which case the Trust may be subjected to penalties imposed by the applicable statutes or the enforceability of the debts may be impaired. Under present Treasury regulations, usurious interest does not qualify as interest under 75 percent or 90 percent income tests referred to in "Taxation—Federal Income Tax."

Possible Disqualifications as a Real Estate Investment Trust

In the event the tax law is changed, the Trust might be disqualified as a real estate investment trust. For a discussion of the consequences of a failure by the Trust at any time to qualify as a real estate investment trust under the Internal Revenue Code, see "Taxation—Federal Income Tax."

Possible Subsequent Offerings

After the completing of this offering the Trust may make subsequent public offerings of Shares or securities convertible into Shares. During such a subsequent offering, which may continue for an extended period of time, broker/dealers who might otherwise make a market in the Shares may be precluded by applicable laws and regulations from doing so if they participate in such subsequent offerings.

Federal Economic Stabilization Policies

Federal fiscal and monetary policies may have a major impact on the availability and cost of funds for development of real estate. The Federal government has the authority to regulate interest rates, rental payments and dividend distributions. Such regulations could have an adverse effect on the Trust.

Environmental Regulations

A number of states, including California, have adopted laws and regulations relating to environmental controls on the development of real estate. Such laws and regulations may operate to reduce the number and attractiveness of investment opportunities available to the Trust.

Experience of Management

The Trust has not yet commenced operations and has no operating history. Certain of the Trustees have no prior experience in managing real estate investment trusts. For a description of the experience of the Trustees and the Directors of the Advisor, see "Management of the Trust" and "The Advisor."

Initial Investments

The Trust may receive offers to acquire equity ownership in exchange for Shares of the Trust and tentative conditional commitments to originate loans for its initial investments.

Lack of Public Market for Shares

There is no present market for the Shares and a shareholder cannot expect to be able to liquidate his investment readily in the case of an emergency. After completion of the offering, the Trust anticipates that a market will develop, but no assurance can be given that such a market will in fact develop or at what price the Shares will trade.

Fiduciary Responsibility of Trustees

The Trustees will bear fiduciary responsibility to the shareholders according to applicable principles of law. In all proceedings connected with the conduct of the business and affairs of the Trust, the Trustees will be bound to act with the highest good faith in all dealings with the shareholders and may not obtain any advantage over them by misrepresentation, concealment, threat or adverse pressure of any kind. Pursuant to such duties, the Trustees will be required to account to the Trust for any benefit or profit jointly and severally or directly or indirectly obtained by them. However, no Trustee or officer of the Trust shall be liable to the Trust or to any Trustee for any act of omission of any other Trustee, shareholder, officer or agent of the Trust or be held to any personal liability whatsoever in tort, contract or otherwise in connection with the affairs of this Trust except only that arising from his own bad faith, willful misconduct, negligence, or reckless disregard of duty. In the event a Trustee breaches his fiduciary duty to the Trust, there is no assurance that legal remedies will be available to the shareholders. The cost of such litigation may be prohibitively high and any judgment obtained may not be collectible.

Minimum Proceeds

In the event the Trust only raises the minimum proceeds, the shareholders' exposure to risk will be increased as the Trust will be unable to diversify its investments to the same degree as if it had greater capital to invest. Further, operating expenses will be proportionately higher and lines of credit more difficult to obtain than if the Trust raises the maximum proceeds.

Adverse Effects of Sale of Advisor

In the event the Directors of the Advisor sell their interest in the Advisor, the purchaser might not have experience in the real estate industry.

Possible Effects of the "Energy Crisis"

The trust is unable to assess the magnitude or seriousness of the "energy crisis" or the effects it might have on the Trust's proposed operation. The Trust is not aware of any specific adverse effect on any of its proposed investment policies.

Managing Stock Exchange Members & Underwriters Is Formed

For the purpose of acting as the underwriter of this offering, Stock Exchange Members & Underwriters has had experience marketing real estate investment trusts. No assurance can be given that this underwriter will be successful in managing this offering.

Potential Conflicts of Interest

The Trustees are not restricted from engaging for their own accounts or for the account of others in business activities of the kinds conducted by the Trust, and situations will arise in which a conflict of interest is involved. Certain of the present Trustees have interests in organizations which may, in the future, be in competition with some of the investment objectives of the Trust. Some of the Directors of the Advisor are currently engaged in various real estate activities. Specifically,

> Jane Roe and John Doe have numerous real estate and development projects in the Moreno Valley and adjacent counties, all located within California; they are both Trustees, licensed Real Estate Brokers, and John Doe is a licensed General Building Contractor engaged in development projects.

The Declaration of Trust permits the Trust to purchase or otherwise acquire property from or sell or otherwise transfer property to an affiliate of a Trustee or participate in a transaction in connection with which an affiliate of a Trustee receives a real estate brokerage commission or other remuneration, but only if each such transaction is approved, after full disclosure of such affiliation by a majority of the Trustees who are not affiliates of any party to such transaction and only if those Trustees determine that such transaction is on terms which are fair and reasonable to the Trust and in event less favorable to the Trust than comparable transactions with others who are not so affiliated. Moreover, any real property so acquired must be at a price (including any real estate brokerage commissions) not more than the fair market value thereof, as determined by independent appraisal, and any real property so sold must be at a price (including any real estate brokerage commissions) at least equal to the fair market value thereof, as determined by an independent appraisal.

The Declaration of Trust requires that the Advisor use its best efforts to present a continuing and suitable investment program to the Trust which is consistent with the investment policies and objectives of the Trust. The Advisor is required to offer to the Trust all investment opportunities that come to it which are within the Trust's investment objectives. The Trustees are not obligated to present any particular investment opportunity to the Trust even if it is of a character which could be taken by the Trust. Subject to the foregoing, any Trustee, Director or affiliate of the Advisor has the right to take for its own account or to recommend to persons other than the Trust any particular investment opportunity. At present neither the Advisor nor any affiliate thereof is engaged in making, investing in or servicing mortgages for its own account or to recommend to persons other than the Trust any particular investment opportunity. At present neither the Advisor nor any affiliate thereof is engaged in making, investing in or servicing mortgages for its own account or for others. Nevertheless, occasions may arise when the interests of the Trust would be in conflict with those of the Advisor or some affiliate of the Advisor. (See "Management of the Trust" and "The Advisor")

The Offering

A total of 5,000,000 Shares, priced at Ten ($10.00) Dollars per Share is offered on a "best efforts" basis through Stock Exchange Members & Underwriters. All subscriptions are payable in cash in full at the time of subscription. No subscriptions will be accepted for other than cash.

Shares may be issued for equity ownership in leaseback and/or purchase transactions.

The Trust reserves the right to reject an offer in whole or part. If a minimum of 100,000 Shares is not sold in this offering within six months from the date of this Prospectus, this offering will terminate and all monies paid by subscribers will promptly be refunded in full with interest earned thereon. If 100,000 Shares or more are sold and the purchase price of such Shares is received by the Trust by that date, this offering may be continued for an additional six months. Subject to the foregoing, the exact date when this offering will terminate and the amount of the Trust's capital upon completion of the offering cannot presently be determined.

Proceeds will be received in trust and within five days from receipt will be deposited in escrow accounts at:

Crocker National Bank   and   Security Pacific National Bank
6301 Beach Blvd.   1633 N. Hacienda Blvd.
Buena Park, CA 90621   La Puente, CA 91747

(or other banking institutions as required or selected)

and will be withdrawn only for the purpose stated in this Prospectus. This account will purchase portions of the Bank's debt securities and additional escrow accounts at various banks to meet the desired or required operational policies.

Plan of Distribution

Solicitation of subscriptions of the Shares will be made on a "best efforts" basis through Stock Exchange Members & Underwriters. Commissions will be payable by the Trust. The Trust will pay sales commissions at the rate of $0.85 per Share at the time the sale is made to underwriter effecting sales.

The Trust has agreed to indemnify soliciting underwriters against certain civil liabilities, including liabilities under the Securities Act of 1933.

Capitalization

The capitalization of the Trust, as of the date of this Prospectus and as adjusted to reflect the sale of the minimum and maximum number of Shares offered hereby, is as follows:

	Outstanding (1)	As Adjusted Assuming 100,000 Shares Sold	As Adjusted Assuming 5,000,000 Shares Sold
Shares of Beneficial Interest ($1.00 par value) (2)	$ 20,000	$120,000	$ 5,020,000
Sales Comm. Fees & Est. Expenses[3]		$(208,500)	$(4,613,500)
Additional Paid in Capital	$ 180,000	$880,000	$44,980,000
	$ 200,000	$791,500	$45,386,500

(1) All of the Shares outstanding on the date of this Prospectus were purchased for or traded at Ten ($10.00) Dollars per Share by First National Advisors, Inc. No selling commissions were paid by the Trust in connection with such sale.
(2) The number of Shares of Beneficial Interest which may be issued by the Trust is unlimited.
(3) After deducting maximum selling commissions at 0.85 percent per Share and other expenses of the offering, estimated to be $200,000 but not to exceed 15 percent of the gross proceeds of this offering.

Borrowing Policy

The Trust anticipates that it will employ borrowed capital to increase its funds available for investment. The Trust will seek bank lines of credit as the need arises. The banks granting such lines of credit may in connection with borrowings thereunder impose restrictions on the Trust's further borrowings and operating policies, may impose conditions as to the minimum net worth, and may require the Trust to maintain compensating balances in the form of non–interest bearing bank accounts. Maintenance of such compensating balances will increase the effective cost of borrowings under such lines. Although lines of credit are not legal commitments, they are traditionally honored by banking institutions. Such lines of credit normally are reviewed annually by the banks for renewal.

The Trust also may issue commercial paper supported by letters of credit or bank lines of credit and may borrow from institutional investors and other lenders. However, the Trust will not pledge any of the proceeds of this offering or any securities, certificates of deposit or other similar investments in which such proceeds may be temporarily invested. The Trust does not contemplate short-term borrowing to obtain funds for long-term investments, although investments financed out of borrowed funds will often have longer maturities than those of the borrowed funds.

The Declaration of Trust prohibits any increase in the outstanding obligations of the Trust for borrowed money unless, after giving effect to the proposed increase, the aggregate indebtedness of the Trust for borrowed money, whether secured or unsecured, will not exceed 500 percent of the

Net Assets of the Trust. However, in the initial years, the Trust does not anticipate that it will be able to borrow an amount greater than 400 percent of its Net Assets. No assurance can be given that the Trust will be able to borrow any amounts. To the extent the Trust is unable to borrow funds, its ability to leverage its investments will be limited. For the purposes of this limitation, Net Assets of the Trust means total assets of the Trust after deducting therefrom any liabilities of the Trust, except that depreciable assets may be included therein at the lesser of either (1) the cost of such assets on the books of the Trust less depreciation thereof, or (2) the fair market value of such assets in the judgment of the Trustees.

The Trustees will not issue debt securities to the public unless the historical cash flow of the Trust or the estimated cash flow of the Trust, excluding extraordinary items, is sufficient in the judgment of the Trustees to cover the interest on such securities.

Use of Proceeds

The net proceeds to the Trust from the sale of the Shares offered hereby and of the 20,000 Shares sold to First National Advisors, Inc., prior to the date of this Prospectus are estimated at a minimum of $791,500 and a maximum of $45,386,500, after deduction of selling commissions and estimated expenses of $200,000 (of which anything in excess of 15 percent of the gross proceeds will be paid by the Advisor) payable by the Trust. Said net proceeds are to be invested as described under "Investment and Operating Policies of the Trust" commencing promptly after a minimum of 100,000 Shares have been sold pursuant to this offering.

All of the net proceeds will be received and held by the Trust in special bank accounts with:

Crocker National Bank	and	Security Pacific National Bank
6301 Beach Blvd.		1633 N. Hacienda Blvd.
Buena Park, CA 90621		La Puente, CA 91747

(and other banks as selected or needed)

and immediately, or from time to time thereafter, will be released from such accounts and transferred from general funds of the Trust to be used only for the purposes described above. In the event 100,000 Shares are not sold prior to six months after the date of this Prospectus, all of the funds received, plus any interest earned thereon, will be returned to the investors.

To the extent that the net proceeds are not immediately invested as described in the preceding paragraph, such funds may be temporarily invested in short-term government securities, certificates of deposit of commercial banks, bankers acceptances, and mortgage-backed securities guaranteed by the Government National Mortgage Association. The rate of return on such investments is likely to be less than will be obtained from mortgage loans and other investments in real property.

Distributions

The Trust intends initially to declare and make cash distributions of 90 percent of its taxable income to shareholders of record on a quarterly basis. However, the Trust may in the future make such distributions on a monthly, rather than a quarterly basis, if the Trustees determine that to do so would be advantageous to the Trust. By distributing annually at least 90 percent of its real estate investment trust taxable income, the Trust will comply with applicable sections of the Internal Revenue Code governing minimum distributions by qualifying real estate investment trusts and, assuming compliance with other requirements, income so distributed will not be taxable to the Trust. Cash distributions in excess of the Trust's net income may also be made at the discretion of the Trustees if cash generated from operations is in excess of net income. Such distributions would constitute a return of capital to the shareholders (insofar as they exceed the cost basis of Shares), and, under existing law, be tax-free to the shareholders at the time of distribution and would result in a corresponding reduction in the cost basis of Shares. Subject to the foregoing, all distributions by the Trust, including distributions of any capital gains by the Trust, will be at the discretion of the Trustees and will depend upon the earnings of the Trust, its financial condition and other relevant factors. The Trust will notify each shareholder as to what portion of any distribution is believed to constitute ordinary income, return of capital or capital gains. (See "Taxation") No assurance can be given that the Trust will pay a cash dividend; however, the Trustees will establish a dividend reinvestment plan if and when dividends are paid. Any such program would comply with Federal and State securities regulations.

Investment and Operating Policies of the Trust

The Trustees intend to provide real estate developers with a broad range of financial borrowing services. The Trust's investments will consist primarily of first mortgage development and construction loans on residential, commercial and industrial real properties anywhere in the United States, its possessions and territories and foreign countries. The Trust may also invest in both permanent ("long-term") and intermediate-term interests in income-producing properties, including interests acquired in purchase-leaseback and net lease financing transactions, permanent first mortgage loans, junior and wrap-around mortgage loans, leasehold mortgage loans and real estate equity investments. The Trust may also make standby and gap loan commitments. Wherever practicable, the Trust will seek additional returns from participation in revenues generated by the properties financed or from equity interests in such properties or other ventures. It is the Trust's primary purpose to acquire assets for income.

The Trustees are authorized, but do not presently intend, to make loans and investments other than the previously described policies. The Trustees, without shareholder approval, reserve the right to effect changes in the Trust's portfolio, by sale or otherwise, within the limitations imposed by the Declaration of Trust, if, in their judgment, such changes are in the best interests of the Trust's shareholders in the light of changes in business and financial conditions and in the application of laws and governmental regulations. The Trustees have the right to change the investment policies of the Trust without shareholder approval. The Trust has the authority to offer its Shares in exchange for investments which conform to its standards, and it intends to do so. The Trustees do not intend to invest in the securities of other issuers for the purpose of exercising control. It is not the policy of the Trust to hold any investments primarily for sale in the ordinary course of business or with a view to making short-term profits from the sale of investments. If the maximum proceeds of this offering are received, the Trust will not invest more than 10 percent of its total assets in any single property; however, if only the minimum proceeds of $1,000,000 are received, the Trust may invest up to one-half of its proceeds in any one property.

Description of Types of Investments

There follows a more detailed description of the characteristics of each of the various types of investments which the Trust may make and of the related policies and other consideration which the Trustees will apply in their operation of the Trust.

Construction Loans

The Trust may make construction loans to finance the construction of properties such as shopping centers, apartment houses, condominiums, resort condominiums and office, commercial and industrial buildings, and single family residential developments. Before a construction loan is made, the Trustees shall determine, based upon the security available for such loan, including personal guarantees, whether it will be a requirement that a commitment be obtained from a responsible financial institution or mortgage banker providing for permanent financing on the completed property. (See "Risk Factors–Short-Term Investment Risks") The Trust will require that the project be constructed in accordance with engineering, architectural and other requirements approved by the Advisor and that the construction be subject to inspection by the Advisor or other qualified persons at various stages and frequently will require that the borrower shall have obtained a satisfactory commitment (which may be from the Trust or from an affiliate of the Advisor) for a long-term first mortgage loan on the completed property. Construction loans will be advanced in installments after periodic inspections indicate satisfactory progress of the project. Construction loans normally do not exceed three (3) years and the Trust will not normally make a construction loan if the balance outstanding thereunder exceeds 80 percent of the appraised value of the completed property.

Development Loans

The Trust may invest in development loans to finance or refinance the acquisition of unimproved land and the installation thereon of utilities, drainage, sewage and road systems. The Trust generally will require that the project be developed in accordance with engineering and other requirements approved by the Trustees, and the loan will be advanced in installments after review of the project's progress by the Advisor. The Trust will not normally require the borrower to obtain a commitment for a construction or long-term mortgage loan on the developed property, although development loan will be normally repaid with the proceeds of subsequent refinancing or the sale of the property. In some instances, the borrower may offer the Trust an equity or other interest in connection with the property being developed. Development loans normally do not exceed three (3) years. The Trust will not normally make a development loan if the balance outstanding thereunder exceeds 75 percent of the appraised value of the property when development is completed.

Purchase-Leaseback Financings

The Trust may invest in purchase-leaseback transactions in which the Trust purchases land and/or the improvements thereon and leases it back, normally to the seller, at a specified rental subject to the condition that said purchases must be limited to no more than 10 percent of the Trust's total assets. The purchase price will not exceed the fair market value of the property. The rentals usually provide for the recovery of the purchase price over the initial term of the lease plus interest on the average unrecovered cost of the property over the initial term. Provision may be made for additional consideration in the form of a participation in gross income derived from, or an equity interest in, the property being financed. The seller/tenant may have options to renew the lease for additional periods after the expiration of the initial term and may have purchase options as to the property. In cases where no purchase options are granted, the Trust will be entitled to the residual value of the property at the expiration of the lease.

In land purchase-leaseback transactions, the Trust will purchase the land underlying the existing or proposed income-producing improvement, typically an apartment project or shopping center, and lease the land to the owner of the improvements thereon. In such cases, the Trust might also make a leasehold mortgage loan on the improvements on the land secured by an assignment of the leasehold estate or may subordinate its fee estate to the lien of the mortgage on the property held by another lender.

Leasehold Mortgage Loans

The Trust may make leasehold mortgage loans on improved real property secured by a lien on the leasehold estate of the borrower in the property. In such cases, the owner of the property may or may not have subordinated the fee estate to the lien of the mortgage. Leasehold mortgage loans will generally have a maturity of from 10 to 30 years (but in no event longer than the leasehold estate), will require level payments sufficient to repay the loan with interest before the expiration of the leasehold estate and normally will not be made if the balance outstanding thereunder exceeds 85 percent of the appraised value of the leasehold estate.

Net Lease Financings

Net lease financings are mortgage loans or purchase-leaseback transactions secured by a long-term lease from a lessee of high credit standing. In such cases, the loan or investment of the Trust may be in an amount equal to 100 percent of the appraised value of the subject property. The lease is generally on a net basis at a rental calculated to repay the loan or investment with interest no later than the end of the term of the lease. Net lease mortgage loans are secured by an assignment of the net lease and by a mortgage on the borrower's interest in the property.

Long-Term Mortgage Loans

The Trust will invest in long-term first mortgage loans with maturities ranging from 10 to 30 years which will ordinarily finance the purchase or ownership of income-producing real property, or interests therein. Long-term first mortgage loans acquired by the Trust will be required to meet the same standards applied to loans of other types acquired by the Trust and will not be made in situations deemed by the Trustees to involve significant risk. It is expected that most of the Trust's permanent mortgage loans will provide for amortization over terms ranging from 15 to 30 years. In making such loans, the Trust may seek a participation in the gross income derived from or an equity interest in the property being financed.

Intermediate-Term Loans

Intermediate-term loans of the type the Trust may make or acquire are mortgage loans on improved properties made primarily for the purpose of permitting a developer to delay obtaining long-term financing for a project with a view to securing more favorable loan terms. The loans normally will be for terms of from two (2) or three (3) years up to seven (7) years, will have interest at rates higher than prevailing rates on long-term loans of comparable quality, will provide for little or no amortization of principal during the term thereof and will be secured by first mortgages.

Junior Mortgage and Wrap-Around Loans

The trust may invest in junior mortgage loans, including wrap-around loans subject to the condition that junior mortgage loans, excluding wrap-around loans, must be limited to no more than 10 percent of the Trust's total assets. Wrap-around loans are defined to mean a junior mortgage loan on real property which is made pursuant to an agreement obligating the borrower to pay to the Trust a combined principal equal to the principal of any senior mortgage loan plus the principal of such junior mortgage loan plus interest on the combined principal and obligating the Trust to pay, as received from the borrower, the principal and interest due on any such senior mortgage loan. The wrap-around lender generally receives level periodic principal and interest payments on the full amount of the wrap-around loan out of which must be deducted the periodic principal and interest payments due on the existing first mortgage loan. The yield to the wrap-around lender may be increased since normally interest is paid on the entire face amount of the wrap-around loan at a rate higher than the rate paid on the first mortgage loan included within the wrap-around loan.

Junior mortgages have higher yields than first mortgage loans, but involve substantially greater risks and are more susceptible to loss due to declines in the value of the underlying property.

Standby and Gap Loan Commitments

The Trust may issue standby commitments which will normally not exceed three (3) years to invest in various permitted investments, including first mortgages on completed construction projects. The first mortgage loan as to which the standby commitment is issued normally will not exceed 25 years and will be required to meet the same standards applied to the acquisition of any similar loan. The Trustees intend to issue such commitments for fees based on the maximum amount of the mortgage.

Institutions usually issue commitments to invest in permanent first mortgages on income-producing properties which contain a provision fixing an unconditional minimum amount (normally 80 to 85 percent of the face amount of the total commitment) above which the institutions will not fund unless certain rental requirements on a construction project are satisfied. The remaining 15 to 20 percent constitutes the "gap" in the commitment and will be funded within an agreed time period after a stipulated rental figure has been achieved. The Trust may from time to time issue commitments covering this gap for fees based on the amount of the Trust's commitment. In the event that the Trust is called upon to fund its gap commitment, the security of its mortgage loan would be subordinate to the lien of the first mortgage on the property.

Standby and gap commitment fees may not be includable in the permitted classes of income in applying the 75 percent test and 1 percent test described in item (2) under "Taxation—Federal Income Taxation."

Real Estate Equity Investments

The Trust may acquire ownership of, or a participation in the ownership of, or rights to acquire, equity interests in all types of income-producing real property such as apartment buildings, shopping centers, office buildings, industrial buildings, mobile home parks, motels, hotels, motor inns, health care facilities, leisure time properties, and recreational properties or in entities owning, developing, improving, financing, operating, or managing real property with a view to providing income and/or capital appreciation. These interests may be in the form of direct ownership, stock, stock purchase warrants, or other interests in such entities. Such interests may be acquired independently of or in connection with other investment activities of the Trust and may include rights to receive additional payments based on gross income or rental income from the property or improvements thereon. Real estate equity investments may be in the form of purchase-leaseback or net lease financing, described above.

The Trust has not formulated any criteria as to the form its ownership interest in real property may take, although it will not enter into joint ventures unless it has a greater than 50 percent interest nor has the Trust established any financial criteria to be met by the entity whose securities the Trust may purchase. The Trustees believe that it is impractical to establish any such criteria in advance of making investments since each investment of this kind must be evaluated on its individual merits. In acquiring an ownership interest in real property, the Declaration of Trust requires an appraisal of the real property, prepared by a qualified, disinterested, independent appraiser, before making such investment, except that the Trust may acquire at cost newly constructed real property which has not been in use for more than one (1) year without an appraisal. Such equity interests will in any event be acquired only if the Trust is satisfied, based upon the opinion of counsel, that such acquisition will not jeopardize the ability of the Trust to qualify as a real estate investment trust under the applicable sections of the Internal Revenue Code (see "Taxation") or cause the Trust to become subject to regulation under the Investment Company Act of 1940. The Trustees do not intend to invest in the securities of other issuers for the purpose of exercising control over such other issuers.

Other Investments

The only restriction as to the forms of real property investments the Trust may make are described in the section titled "Taxation." Such investments may incorporate a variety of real property financing techniques such as purchase and installment salebacks, convertible mortgages, and mortgages of special interest, such as condominiums and air rights, and may include subsequently developed financing techniques not otherwise prohibited.

To the extent the assets are not invested in the investments described above and subject to the prohibitions referred to above, the Trust may invest in loans secured by the pledge of mortgages on real property, securities of other entities (including securities of other real estate investment trusts), government securities and certificates of deposit.

Certain Operating Policies

The Trust has the authority to offer Shares and other securities of the Trust in exchange for investments which conform to its standards, and it intends to do so. It is not the policy of the Trust to hold any investment primarily for sale in the ordinary course of business or with a view of making short-term profits from the sale of investments.

When the obligor to the Trust is in default under the terms of any obligation (including the obligation to pay rent) to the Trust, the Trustees shall have the power to pursue any remedies permitted by law which in their sole judgment are in the interest of the Trust and the Trustees shall have the power to receive and to hold any investment and to enter into any commitment or obligation on behalf of the Trust in connection with or in pursuit of such remedies, which in the judgment of the Trustees, is necessary or desirable for the purpose of acquiring and disposing of property acquired in the pursuit of such remedies.

The Declaration of Trust does not limit the location of real property in which the Trust may invest. The Trustees will seek to invest the Trust's assets in geographic areas where the most favorable yields prevail commensurate with their judgment of the risks involved.

The Declaration of Trust specifies that the Trustees need not give bond, but it will be the policy of the Trust to require bonding, in amounts considered by the Trustees to be adequate, of officers, employees and agents and of Trustees when undertaking duties beyond those of Trustees.

The Trustees intend to establish a reserve for possible loan losses in an amount which, in their judgment, will be adequate in terms of the number, amount and nature of the loans for which the Trust may be committed. Initially, this reserve will be no less than 15 percent of the Trust's net income before provision for the reserve.

The Trust will not: invest in commodities, foreign currencies, bullion or chattels except as required in the operation of the Trust; invest in any contracts for the sale of real estate in excess of a value of one (1) percent of the total assets of the Trust estate; engage in any material trading activities or in any short sale; issue "redeemable securities"; borrow money, if, after giving effect to any proposed increase in the aggregate principal amount of outstanding obligations of the Trust for borrowed money, the aggregate principal amount of all such obligations of the Trust for borrowed money, including non-recourse indebtedness of the Trust, shall not exceed 500 percent of the net assets of the Trust; invest more than 10 percent of the total assets of the Trust in unimproved real property or mortgage loans on unimproved real property, excluding property which is being developed or which the Trustees reasonably expect will be developed within three (3) years; hold equity securities issued by any person which to the actual knowledge of the Trustees is then holding investments or engaging in activities prohibited to the Trustees; provided, however, that the foregoing limitation shall not apply to (i) equity securities acquired through foreclosure of a mortgage held by the Trust or acquired in connection with the making of a mortgage loan if the Trust gives no consideration other than the making of such loan, and (ii) equity securities held by the Trust representing not more than 5 percent of the total assets of the trust estate issued by a person who, at the time of acquisition of such equity securities derives not less than 95 percent of its gross income from any one or more of the following activities: acquisition, development, management or sale of real property, issue equity securities of more than one class (other than convertible obligations, warrants, rights and options); issue debt securities to the public unless the historical cash flow of the Trust or the estimated future cash flow of the Trust, excluding extraordinary items, is sufficient, in the judgment of the Trustees to cover the interest on such debt securities; issue options or warrants to purchase securities of the Trust to the Advisor or any person who is an affiliate of the Advisor, except as part of an issuance to all shareholders ratably or pursuant to a public offering, or to any other person at exercise prices less than the fair market value of such securities at the time of the grant, except as part of a public offering or other financing by the Trust or an issuance to all shareholders ratably; invest more than 10 percent of the total assets of the Trust in junior mortgage loans, exclusive of wrap-around loans and junior mortgage loans where the Trust also holds the first mortgage loan; engage in the underwriting or agency distribution of securities issued by others; invest in share of other real estate investments trusts; and invest more than 10 percent of the total assets of the Trust in leasehold interests.

Initial Investments

The Trust intends to invest the proceeds of this offering in the western United States, especially southern California area, but no assurance can be given as to the total amount that will be invested since the Trust is obligated to invest its capital in geographical areas for the best returns on those investments commensurate with the risks involved. Tentative commitments will be supplied by the Trust to the Securities and Exchange Commission during registration. No firm commitments will be made until a tentative schedule for Registration approval is complete and sales of the required 100,000 shares of stock has been made.

MANAGEMENT OF THE TRUST

The Trustees and principal officers of the Trust are:

NAME	PRINCIPAL OCCUPATIONS AND AFFILIATIONS
JOHN DOE Trustee and President of the Trust, Executive Committee Member	[Résumé]
JANE ROE Trustee and Vice President of the Trust, Executive Committee Member	[Résumé]
DOE TWO Trustee and Secretary	[Résumé]
DOE THREE Trustee and Treasurer	[Résumé]

NAME	PRINCIPAL OCCUPATIONS AND AFFILIATIONS
DOE FOUR Trustee, Executive Committee Member	[Résumé]
DOE FIVE Trustee, Executive Committee Member	[Résumé]
DOE SIX Trustee	[Résumé]

    The Trustees, or their nominees, will hold legal title to the property of the Trust.

    The Trustees are responsible for the general policies of the Trust and for such general supervision of the business of the Trust conducted by all officers, agents, employees, advisors, managers or independent contractors of the Trust as may be necessary to insure that such business conforms to the provisions of the Declaration of Trust. However, the Trustees are not and shall not be required personally to conduct the business of the Trust and, consistent with their ultimate responsibility as stated above, the Trustees shall have the power to appoint, employ or contract with any persons (including one or more of themselves or any affiliate of any of them) as the Trustees may deem necessary or proper for the transaction of the business of the Trust. It is estimated that John Doe and Jane Roe spend substantially all of their time on the business of the Trust; Attorney XYZ shall spend 5 percent of his time on Trust business, and the remaining Trustees less than 10 percent of their time on Trust business.

    In order to obtain for the Trust services of individuals having substantial experience in such areas as finance and real estate, the Declaration of Trust does not restrict the other business activities of any Trustee, officer or employee of the Trust. Such persons are free to engage and in some cases engage in other business activities related to real estate investments, some of which are competitive with the business of the Trust, and generally they shall not have any obligation to present to the Trust any investment opportunities which may come to them, regardless of whether such opportunities are within the Trust's investment policies.

The Trustees and officers of the Trust will each devote such time to the affairs of the Trust as needed to fulfill their respective duties but are not expected to spend a substantial portion of their time on trust business. It is anticipated that Trustees will receive $20,000 per year, payable quarterly, plus $100 per Trustees' meeting attended, plus a reimbursement of any costs incurred in connection with meetings attended. As the Trustees will not be devoting full time to the management of the Trust, the Trust will operate through an executive committee of five (5) Trustees, who have the authority to execute the Board of Trustees' approved Trust investments. The executive committee members shall receive, in addition to Trustee compensation, additional income of $32,000 per year maximum for devoting required time to those required Executive Committee activities.

The Advisor

The Advisor of the Trust is First National Advisors, Inc., a corporation, which has no experience with real estate investment trust matters. However, the Directors of the Advisors have had experience in real estate and syndications, financing, sales and real estate development.

Jane Roe and John Doe are licensed Real Estate Brokers, and John Doe is a licensed General Building Contractor, and both are licensed Security and Exchange Representatives and all Advisors will be licensed by the Security and Exchange Commission.

The Directors and Associates of the Advisor will devote such time as necessary to fulfill their obligations under the Advisory Agreement. It is anticipated that John Doe and Jane Roe will spend substantially all of their time on the activities of the Trust; XYZ, Legal Counsel, will spend five (5) percent of his time on these activities, while other partners of the Advisor will spend less than ten (10) percent of their time on the Activities of the Trust.

John Doe and Jane Roe may be deemed to be promoters of the Trust.

Advisory Agreement

The Trust has entered into an Advisory Agreement with the Advisor for services as an investment advisor to the Trust. The original term is for a period of three (3) years, commencing upon the close of escrow of the first 100,000 Shares sold pursuant to this offering. Successive extensions, each for one year only, may be made by agreement between the parties. The Agreement is assignable only with the consent of both the Trust and the Advisor, except that the Advisor may assign the Agreement without the Trust's consent to a corporation, partnership or other successor organizations which control, are controlled by, or are under common control with the Advisor or any of its shareholders which may take over and carry on the affairs of the Advisor. The Agreement, or any extension thereof, may be terminated at any time on 90 days' written notice by a majority of the disinterested Trustees or the shareholders of the Trust or by the Directors of the Advisor, without penalty.

The Advisor is at all times subject to the supervision of the Trustees and has only such authority as the Trust may delegate to it as its agent. The Trustees may confer broad administrative powers on the Advisor, who shall perform such research and investigation as the Trustees may request in connection with the policy decisions as to the type and nature of investments to be made by the Trust, including the evaluation of the desirability of acquisition, retention and disposition of specific Trust assets. The Advisor may also be responsible for the day-to-day investment operations of the Trust and will conduct relations with mortgage loan brokers, originators and servicers, and will determine whether loans offered to the Trust meet the requirements of the Trust. In addition to the general duties, the Advisor intends to provide a substantial amount of the requisite servicing of the Trust's mortgage loans. (See "The Advisor—Compensation Provisions")

The Agreement provides that Directors, associates, and employees of the Advisor and its affiliates may serve as Trustees, officers, employees, agents, attorneys, nominees and signatories for the Trust.

Compensation Provisions

The Agreement provides that the Advisor shall receive as its regular compensation a monthly fee of 4/50 of 1 percent (.96 percent per annum) of the "average book value of the Invested Assets" of the Trust. "Invested Assets" is defined as the "Total Assets" of the Trust, plus the undisbursed commitments in respect of closed loans and other closed investments, but excluding goodwill and other intangible assets, cash, cash items and obligations of municipal, state and Federal governments and governmental agencies (other than obligations secured by a lien on real property owned, or to be acquired, by such governments or governmental agencies and securities of other governmental agencies issuing securities backed by a pool of mortgages). "Total Assets" of the Trust is defined as the value of all of the assets of the Trust estate as such value appears on the most recent balance sheet of the Trust available to the Trustees without deduction for mortgage loans or other security interests to which such assets are subject and before provision for depreciation, depletion, and amortization, but after provision for bad debt loss and similar reserves.

The Agreement also provides for incentive compensation for each fiscal year of the Trust in an amount equal to the sum of 10 percent of the realized capital gains (net of accumulated net realized capital losses) and extraordinary non-recurring items of income of the Trust for such fiscal year, plus 10 percent of the amount, if any, by which Net Profits of the Trust for such fiscal year exceed 10 percent per annum of the average net worth of the Trust during such year. The term "Net Profits" is defined in the Advisory Agreement as the gross earned income of the Trust (exclusive of capital gains and extraordinary non-recurring items of income) after all expenses (including bad debts written off), except reserves required to be set aside from earnings, the incentive compensation payable to the Advisor and any taxes on the Trust's income.

If and to the extent that the Trust shall request the Advisor, or any of its Directors, officers, or employees, to render services for the Trust other than those required to be rendered by the Advisor under the Agreement, such additional services shall be compensated separately on terms to be agreed upon between such party and the Trust from time to time, which terms shall be fair and reasonable and at least as favorable to the Trust as similar arrangements for comparable transactions of which the Trust is aware with organizations unaffiliated with the Advisor.

Under the Agreement, the Advisor is obligated to refund to the Trust all or part of the Advisor's compensation otherwise payable each year up to the amount, if any, by which Operating Expenses, as defined, of the Trust during that fiscal year, exceed the lesser of (a) 1-1/2 percent of the average monthly book value of the Invested Assets of the Trust for such year, or (b) the greater of (i) 1-1/2 percent of the average month-end Net Assets of the Trust Estate for such fiscal year, or (ii) 25 percent of the Trust's Net Income for such year excluding extraordinary items and realized capital gains and losses from the disposition of assets of the Trust and before deducting regular and incentive advisory fees and servicing fees and expenses and depreciation. "Net Income" for any period means the net income of the Trust for such period computed on the basis of its results of operations for such period, after deduction of all expenses (other than compensation paid to the Advisor and fees payable to mortgage servicers) and excluding extraordinary items and gains and losses from the disposition of assets of the Trust. "Operating Expenses" shall mean the aggregate annual expenses of the Trust of every character regarded as operating expenses in accordance with generally accepted accounting principles, as determined by independent accountants selected by the Trustees, exclusive of: the cost of borrowed money; taxes on income and taxes and assessments on real property and all other taxes applicable to the Trust; legal, audit, accounting, underwriting, brokerage, registration and other fees, printing, engraving and other expenses and taxes incurred in connection with the issuance, distribution and transfer of the Trust's securities; expenses connected with the acquisition, disposition and ownership of real estate interests or mortgage loans or other property including the costs of foreclosure, insurance premiums (except premiums for Trustee's liability insurance), legal services, brokerage and sales commissions, maintenance, repair and improvement of property; expenses of maintaining and managing real estate equity interests and processing and servicing (but excluding the cost of supervision thereof by the Advisor) mortgage, development, construction and other loans; insurance as required by the Trustees; the expenses of organizing or terminating the Trust; expenses connected with payments of dividends or interest or distributions in cash or any other form made or caused to be made by the Trustees to holders of securities of the Trust; all expenses connected with communications to holders of securities of the Trust and other bookkeeping and clerical work necessary in maintaining relations with holders of securities, including the cost of printing and mailing certificates for securities and proxy solicitation materials and reports to holders of the Trust's securities; the cost of annual audits; and fees and charges of transfer agents, registrars, warrant agents and indenture trustees.

With respect to the above, legal, inspection, title insurance, mortgage and conveyance taxes, architectural supervision and similar fees related to investments of the Trust are generally borne in whole or in part by the borrower or seller of property to the Trust. It is anticipated that the Advisor and/or its affiliates may provide some of these services. In any given fiscal year of the Trust, the Advisor or its affiliates may receive from parties other than the Trust a real estate brokerage commission in connection with the purchase or sale of Trust assets (no such commission being payable by the Trust). The advisory Agreement provides that the compensation otherwise payable by the Trust to the Advisor in that fiscal year shall be reduced by an amount equal to the amount of such commission received by the Advisor or its affiliates, but not exceeding an amount equal to 100 percent of such compensation otherwise payable in that fiscal year to the Advisor by the Trust. (See "Summary of Declaration of Trust—Affiliated Transactions")

The preceding summary of certain provisions of the Advisory Agreement is qualified in its entirety by reference to the full text of such Agreement, a copy of which is filed as an exhibit to the Registration Statement of which this Prospectus is a part.

Sale of Securities of the Advisor

The Declaration of Trust and Advisory Agreement further provide that no holder of securities of the Advisor (including any such holder who is in control of the Advisor) shall be prohibited for any reason from transferring directly or indirectly all or any portions of such securities by sale, exchange or otherwise, or shall be required to obtain the consent of the Trust, or any of its shareholders, for such a transfer; neither the Trust nor its shareholders shall have or shall exercise any rights in or with respect to income or profits realized by any such security holder by reason of any such direct or indirect transfer; and by purchasing Shares, each shareholder shall be deemed to have consented to any such transfer and to have expressly and irrevocably waived any interest in or rights with respect to any such income or profits from a transfer of securities of the Advisor whether arising under the laws or regulations of the United States or any state or territory thereof, or under any judicial decision at law or in equity. Thus, under the terms of the Declaration of Trust and Advisory Agreement, the Advisor would be permitted to sell or otherwise dispose of all or any portion of its securities while the Advisory Agreement is still in effect without the Trust or its shareholders having an interest in any income or profits therefrom.

The question has been raised by counsel as to the applicability to real estate investment trusts of a recent legal decision handed down with respect to mutual funds registered under the Investment Company Act of 1940. If this decision should be held applicable to the Trust, any profit realized from the sale of securities of the Advisor would have to be paid over to the Trust. The provision of the Declaration of Trust summarized above is designed to make this decision inapplicable to the sale of securities of the Advisor and is intended to constitute a waiver of any claim which the Trust or its shareholders might have to any such profit. There can be no assurance, however, that this waiver is binding upon the Trust's shareholders or enforceable under the Federal securities laws or under the law of California.

Taxation

Federal Income Tax

During this first interim fiscal period, the Trust will endeavor to operate in such a manner as to qualify as a real estate investment trust under Sections 856–858 of the Internal Revenue Code, but no assurance can be given that it will so qualify. Under such Sections, a real estate investment trust which in any taxable year meets certain requirements will not be subject to Federal income tax with respect to income which it distributes to shareholders other than with respect to certain "items of tax preference" which may subject the Trust to the "minimum tax" imposed by Section 56 of the Internal Revenue Code.

To qualify to be taxed as a real estate investment trust under the Internal Revenue Code, the Trust must elect to be so treated and must meet the following requirements, among others:

(1) At the end of each fiscal quarter, at least 75 percent of the value of the total assets of the Trust must consist of real estate assets (real property, interests in mortgages on real property and shares in other qualified real estate investment trusts), cash, cash items and govern-

ment securities. No more than 25 percent of the value of the Trust's total assets may be represented by non-government securities which do not qualify as real estate assets. With respect to non-government securities acquired by the Trust of any one issuer, such securities may not represent more than 5 percent of the value of the Trust's total assets or more than 10 percent of the outstanding voting securities of such issuer.

(2) At least 75 percent of the gross income of the Trust for the taxable year must be derived from rents from real property, interest on obligations secured by mortgages on real property or on interests in real property, gains from the disposition of real estate assets, dividends or other qualified real estate investment trusts and abatements and refunds of real estate taxes. For purposes of the foregoing, rents from real property do not include: (i) amounts with respect to any real property if the Trust furnishes services to the tenants of such property other than through an independent contractor, (ii) amounts measured by the profits of a tenant, or (iii) amounts received from a tenant in which the Trust has a 10 percent or greater proprietary interest. Only that portion of rent received under leases covering both real and personal property which is properly allocable to the real property will qualify as rent. An additional 15 percent of the Trust's gross income must be derived from these same sources or from other dividends, other interest, or gains from the disposition of other stock or securities.

(3) Gross income for the taxable year from the disposition of stock or securities held for less than six (6) months and of real property held for less than four (4) years must comprise less than 30 percent of the gross income of the Trust.

(4) The Trust may not hold any property primarily for sale to customers in the ordinary course of its trade or business.

(5) Beneficial ownership of the Trust must be held by 100 or more persons during at least 335 days of a taxable year of twelve (12) months or during a proportionate part of a shorter taxable year. More than 50 percent of the value of the outstanding shares (including in some circumstances shares into which outstanding securities might be converted) may not be owned actually or constructively (within the meaning of Section 544 of the Internal Revenue Code) by or for five (5) or fewer individuals at any time during the last half of any taxable year. Each year the Trust must demand written statements from the

record holders of designated percentages of its Shares, disclosing the actual and constructive owners of such Shares, and must maintain within the internal revenue district in which it is required to file its federal income tax return permanent records showing the information it has thus received as to the actual ownership of such Shares, and a list of those persons failing or refusing to comply with such demand.

(6) The Trust must distribute to shareholders at least 90 percent of its real estate investment trust taxable income (taxable income excluding the excess of net long-term capital gains over net short-term capital losses, and otherwise adjusted as provided in Section 857 of the Internal Revenue Code), computed without regard to the deduction allowed for dividends paid to shareholders.

In any year in which the Trust qualifies to be taxed as a real estate investment trust it will not be taxed on that portion of its ordinary income or capital gain which is distributed to shareholders except for a possible "minimum tax" on certain "items of tax preference." However, the Trust will be taxed at applicable corporate rates on any undistributed taxable income or capital gain and the shareholders will be taxed on this income if it is distributed to them as dividends. The Trust will not be entitled to carry back or carry forward any net operating losses.

So long as the Trust qualifies for taxation as a real estate investment trust, distributions made to its shareholders out of current or accumulated earnings and profits will be taxed to them as ordinary income or long-term capital gain, as the case may be. Cash distributions in excess of the Trust's accumulated and current earnings and profits will constitute a return of capital to the shareholder (except insofar as they exceed the cost basis of his Share) and under existing law will be tax-free to the shareholder at the time of distribution and will result in a corresponding reduction in the cost basis of his Shares. The Trust will notify each shareholder as to what portions of the distributions, in the opinion of counsel, constitute ordinary income, return of capital and capital gain. Distributions will not be eligible for the $100 dividend exclusion for individuals or for the 85 percent dividends-received deduction for corporations. Should the Trust incur losses, shareholders will not be entitled to include such losses in their individual income tax returns.

Long-term capital gains distributed by the Trust (like long-term capital gains generally) must be taken into account by the shareholders for the purpose of determining their liability for the 10 percent minimum tax on items of tax preference imposed in Section 56 of the Internal Revenue Code, while undistributed capital gains and certain deductions, including depreciation, if any, in excess of straight-line depreciation, may subject the Trust to such minimum tax liability. The Trust will notify each shareholder as to the amount of such items of tax preference (if any) that must be taken into account for purposes of the minimum tax.

While the Trust intends at all times to operate so as to qualify as a real estate investment trust under the Internal Revenue Code, if in any taxable year it should not so qualify, distributions to its shareholders would not be deductible by the Trust in computing its taxable income, with the result that the assets of the Trust and amounts available for distribution to shareholders would be reduced to the extent of any such tax payable. Such distributions, to the extent made out of the Trust's current or accumulated earnings and profits, would be taxable to the shareholders as dividends but would be eligible for the $100 dividend exclusion for individuals and the 85 percent dividends-received deduction for corporations. Further, because of distributions to shareholders made prior to a determination of the applicability of such tax treatment, the Trust might have to dispose of some of its assets in order to pay such tax.

The foregoing, while summarizing some of the more significant provisions of the Internal Revenue Code which govern the tax treatment of the Trust, is general in character. For a complete statement, reference should be made to the pertinent sections of the Internal Revenue Code and the regulations promulgated thereunder, or shareholders should consult their personal tax counsel.

In the opinion of Mr. XYZ, Attorney at Law, the contemplated method of operation of the Trust complies with the requirements of the Internal Revenue Code for qualification as a real estate investment trust provided the applicable limitations and requirements referred to under this caption are met. The regulations of the Treasury Department require that the Trustees have continuing exclusive authority over the management of the Trust, the conduct of its affairs and, with certain limitations, the management and disposition of the Trust property. It is the intention of the Trustees to effect any amendments to the Declaration of Trust that may be necessary in the opinion of counsel for the Trust to meet the requirements of any modification or interpretation of the regulations. Provisions for such amendment by the Trustees, without the vote or consent of the

Shareholders, is contained in the Declaration of Trust. (See "Summary of Declaration of Trust—Amendment and Termination of the Trust")

State Taxes

In the opinion of Mr. XYZ, Attorney at Law, in any year that the Trust qualifies as a real estate investment trust for federal income tax purposes under Section 856 of the Internal Revenue Code, it will be entitled to a deduction from income taxable under California law equal to the amount of income distributed to its shareholders during each year.

The Trust may be subject to state or local taxes in other jurisdictions in which the Trust may be deemed to be doing business or in which properties securing loans by the Trust are located. In addition, some states may differ from federal income tax treatment.

Description of Shares

The Shares of the Trust are of one class and have a par value of $1.00 per Share. There is no limit on the number of Shares the Trust is authorized to issue. All Shares participate equally in distributions when and as declared by the Trustees and in net assets on liquidation. The Shares do not have any preference, conversion, exchange, preemptive, appraisal or redemption rights, but the Trust may restrict the transfer of, and may redeem, Shares under the circumstances described in "Summary of Declaration of Trust—Redemption and Restrictions on Transfer." The Shares offered pursuant to this Prospectus will be fully paid and non-assessable upon issuance.

The Declaration of Trust provides that the annual meetings of shareholders will be held within six (6) months after the end of each fiscal year commencing with the fiscal year ending in 1983, and special meetings of the shareholders may be called by any two (2) of the Trustees or upon the written request of the holders of 20 percent or more of the outstanding Shares. At any meeting of shareholders, each shareholder is entitled to one (1) vote for each Share owned, and in voting for the election of Trustees, shareholders may cumulate their votes. In addition to voting for the election of Trustees, shareholders may vote on the sale or disposition of more than 50 percent of the assets of the Trust and on such other matters as deemed advisable by the Trustees. It is not anticipated that they will be requested to vote on operational aspects of the Trust. Shareholders may vote by proxy provided that proxies shall have been placed on file with the Trust before the time of voting.

With certain exceptions, Shares are transferable in the same manner as the shares of a California business corporation. (See "Summary of Declaration of Trust—Redemption and Restrictions on Transfer") Initially the Trust will act as its own Transfer Agent.

Holders of Shares of the Trust

As of the date of this Prospectus, there are issued and outstanding 20,000 Shares of the Trust, all of which are owned of record and beneficially by First National Advisors, Inc. Such Shares were purchased or exchanged directly from the Trust prior to and not as part of the offering of Shares made by this Prospectus, and were purchased at a price of $10 per Share, for an aggregate payment to the Trust of $200,000. The Advisor anticipates that one year after the effective date of this Prospectus it may file a registration statement with the Securities and Exchange Commission which will enable it to sell these Shares to the public. In the event the maximum number of Shares offered hereunder is not sold, the market may be adversely affected by the sale of these Shares.

Summary of Declaration of Trust

The following is a summary of the principal provisions of the Declaration of Trust which are not described elsewhere in this Prospectus:

Trustees

The Trustees, subject to specific limitations in the Declaration of Trust and those imposed by law (a majority of which may not be affiliated with the Advisor), have full, exclusive and absolute power, control and authority over the property and business of the Trust. The Trustees named under "Management of the Trust" will serve until the first annual meeting of shareholders to be held within six (6) months after the end of the fiscal year which ends in 1983. Thereafter, the term of each Trustee elected by the shareholders shall continue until the next annual meeting of shareholders. A Trustee may be removed at a special meeting of shareholders by a vote of the holders of a majority of the Shares or by the vote or written consent of all Trustees other than the Trustee whose removal is being considered. Any vacancies in the office of trustee may be filled by a majority of the Trustees continuing in office or by the vote of a majority of the Shares at a meeting called for such purpose, and any Trustee so elected shall hold office until the next annual meeting of shareholders. The number of Trustees shall not be less than seven (7), nor more than ten (10). Initially, there will be seven (7) Trustees. (See "Management of the Trust")

No person shall qualify to serve as Trustee until he shall have signed the Declaration of Trust or agreed in writing to be bound by it. The Declaration of Trust provides that no bond shall be required to secure the performance of a Trustee.

The Trustees are empowered to fix the compensation of all officers and Trustees of the Trust. Under the Declaration of Trust, Trustees may receive reasonable compensation for their services as Trustees and officers of the Trust, and reimbursement of their expenses, and the Trust may pay a Trustee such compensation for special services, including legal services, as the Trustees deem reasonable. The Trustees may delegate any of their powers to an Executive Committee which must be comprised of at least three (3) Trustees who are unaffiliated with any investment advisor of the Trust.

Affiliated Transactions

The Declaration of Trust provides that, with certain exceptions, the Trustees shall not knowingly, directly or indirectly, lend any of the Trust estate to, or purchase or otherwise acquire any property whatsoever (except securities of the Trust) from, or sell or otherwise transfer any property whatsoever (except securities of the Trust) to: any Trustee, officer or employee of the Trust (acting in his individual capacity or otherwise); or the Advisor or any officer, partner or employee (acting in his individual capacity or otherwise) of the Advisor, or any affiliate of the Advisor or Trustee or of any independent contractor of the Trust. For purposes of this section, the term "independent contractor" means an "independent contractor" as defined in Section 856(d)(3) of the Internal Revenue Code, which furnishes or renders services to tenants or manages or operates real property owned by the Trust. Notwithstanding anything in this section to the contrary, the simultaneous acquisition by the Trust and another entity of participation in a loan or other investment shall not be deemed to constitute the purchase or sale of property by one of them to the other, notwithstanding the fact that one of the parties shall have committed to take the entire amount of the loan or investment or the total participation therein to be taken by both such entities for its own account, if the commitment to acquire such loan or investment is assigned to the Trust, in whole or in part, prior to any advance of funds with respect to such loan or investment by the lender or investor under such commitment; and the Trust may make construction or development loans or other short-term investments where an affiliate of the Trust has a commitment to provide the long-term financing, and may make investments in real property on which an affiliate of the Trust has an existing mortgage or other encumbrance. Subject only to the foregoing prohibitions relating to acquisition and disposition of assets and loans, the Trust may enter into any type of transaction or contract with any person, including any one or more Trustees, officers, employees, the Advisor, its partners, officers or employees or any independent contractor of the Trust, and may authorize such amount and type of compensation, including commissions and fees as the Trustees may determine; provided, however, that transactions or contracts with any Trustee or persons who are affiliates of any Trustee or Advisor shall be authorized or subsequently ratified, after disclosure of such interest, by a majority of the Trustees not so interested.

  The Declaration of Trust further provides that the aggregate advisory fees which the Trust is otherwise obligated to pay to the Advisor in any given fiscal year shall be reduced by an amount equal to the amount of any commissions or other compensation or remuneration paid by the Trust to an affiliate of the Advisor in said fiscal year, if and only if, a similar reduction in advisory fees would have been occasioned if said commissions or other compensation or remuneration had been earned by and paid directly to the Advisor by the Trust.

For these purposes, the term "affiliate" shall mean, as to any corporation, partnership or trust, any person: (i) who holds beneficially, directly or indirectly, one percent or more of the outstanding capital stock, shares or equity interests of such corporation, partnership or trust; or (ii) of which one percent or more of its outstanding capital stock, shares or equity interests are held beneficially, directly or indirectly, by such corporation, partnership or trust; or (iii) who directly or indirectly controls, is controlled by, or is under common control with, such corporation, partnership or trust; or (iv) who is an officer, director, employee, partner or trustee of such corporation, partnership or trust, or of any person that controls, is controlled by, or is under common control with such corporation, partnership or trust. For purposes of this paragraph, the Advisor is deemed to be an affiliate of the Trust. (See "Conflicts of Interest" and "The Advisor—Compensation Provisions")

Responsibility of Trustees, Officers and Employees

The Declaration of Trust provides that no Trustee, officer or employee of the Trust will be liable to the Trust, a shareholder or a third party in connection with the affairs of the Trust, except for his own bad faith, willful misfeasance, negligence or reckless disregard of his duties. All third persons must look solely to the Trust property for satisfaction of claims arising in connection with the affairs of the Trust. The Declaration of Trust provides that the Trust may indemnify any present or former Trustee, officer or employee against expense or liability in an action brought by a third party against such person if the remaining Trustees determine that he was acting in good faith within what he reasonably believed to be the scope of his employment or authority and for a purpose which he reasonably believed to be in the best interests of the Trust or its shareholders; and indemnity of any such person for his reasonable expenses may be assessed against the Trust by a court in any proceeding arising out of his alleged misfeasance or nonfeasance or wrongful act against the Trust if the person sued is successful in whole or in part, or the proceeding against him is settled.

Sale of Securities

The Trustees may in their discretion issue Shares or other securities of the Trust for cash, property or other consideration on such terms as they deem advisable, except that the Declaration of Trust provides that options or warrants to purchase securities of the Trust may be issued only at exercise prices not less than the fair market value of such securities at the time of granting of the options or warrants, except as part of a public offering or other financing by the Trust or a ratable issue to shareholders of the Trust's securities, and options or warrants may not be issued to an investment advisor to the Trust or to any affiliate of such an investment advisor unless as a part of an issuance to all shareholders ratably or pursuant to a public offering.

Redemption and Restrictions on Transfer

Under the Internal Revenue Code, one of the requirements for qualification as a real estate investment trust is that, during the last half of the taxable year, not more than 50 percent of the outstanding shares may be owned by five (5) or fewer individuals. In order to meet this requirement, the Trustees are given power to redeem a sufficient number of Shares to bring the ownership of the Shares of the Trust into conformity with the requirements of the Internal Revenue Code, or to prevent the transfer of Shares in order to prevent the ownership of Shares from being concentrated to an extent which may prevent the Trust from qualifying as a real estate investment trust under the Internal Revenue Code. The redemption price to be paid will be the fair market value as reflected in the latest quotations, or, if no quotations are available, as determined in good faith by the Trustees. From and after the date fixed for redemption by the Trustees, the holder of any Shares so called for redemption shall cease to be entitled to any distributions, voting rights and other benefits with respect to the Shares called for redemption except only the right to payment of the redemption price. Under certain circumstances the proceeds of redemptions may be taxed as a dividend to the recipient.

In order to insure that the Trust remains qualified to be taxed as a real estate investment trust once requirements for such qualifications are met, the Declaration of Trust further provides that any transfer of Shares that would prevent the Trust from continuing to be qualified as a real estate investment trust shall be void, and the intended transferee of such Shares shall be deemed to have acted as agent on behalf of the Trustees in acquiring such Shares, and to hold such Shares, on behalf of the Trustees.

Other Restrictions

The Trust shall not issue equity securities redeemable at the option of the holder or equity securities or more than one class (which shall not prohibit the issuance of convertible obligations or, in the case of financings and pro rata distributions to shareholders, warrants, rights and options). Nor will the Trust issue debt securities to the public unless the historical or estimated future cash flow of the Trust, excluding extraordinary items, is sufficient, in the judgment of the Trustees, to cover the interest on the debt securities. The Trust will not underwrite the securities of other issuers.

The Trustees, without approval of the shareholders, may alter the Trust's investment policies, in the light of changes in economic circumstances and other relevant factors, subject to the investment restrictions set forth in the Declaration of Trust.

Reports to Shareholders and Rights of Examination

The Trustees are required to and will furnish annually to the shareholders a report of the Trust, including financial statements, containing a balance sheet, a statement of income and a statement of changes in financial position, examined by an independent certified public accountant prepared in accordance with generally accepted accounting principles. The Trust has retained Deloitte, Haskins & Sells as its independent accountants. The shareholders may for proper purposes inspect the books and records of the Trust during normal business hours at its office.

Amendment and Termination of the Trust

The Declaration of Trust may be amended or altered or the Trust may be terminated by the affirmative written consent or vote of the holders of a majority of the outstanding Shares. The Trustees may amend the Declaration of Trust without the assent of shareholders to the extent the Trustees deem necessary to bring it into conformity with the applicable requirements of the Internal Revenue Code and the regulations thereunder. Notwithstanding the foregoing, no amendment may be made by the shareholders or the Trustees which would change any rights with respect to any outstanding Shares of the Trust by reducing the amount payable thereon upon liquidation of the Trust or by diminishing or eliminating any voting rights pertaining thereto, except with the vote or consent of the holders of two-thirds of the outstanding Shares entitled to vote thereon. The affirmative written consent or vote of the holders of a majority of the outstanding Shares is required to approve the principal terms of the transaction and the nature and amount of the consideration involving any sale, exchange or other disposition of more than 50 percent of the Trust property in any single sale or by multiple sales in the same 12 month period.

Advisor

The Declaration of Trust contains various provisions, including the limitations on compensation required by certain State securities rules and regulations applicable to real estate investment trusts relating to the employment by the Trust of an Advisor. (See "The Advisor")

Duration

The Trust will continue, unless terminated as described above, until the expiration of 20 years after the death of the last survivor of certain living persons of the original Charter Trustees.

The summaries of provisions of the Declaration of Trust set forth above and elsewhere in this Prospectus do not purport to be complete, and reference is made to the Declaration of Trust filed as an exhibit to the Registration Statement for the complete provisions of such Declaration, and the summaries herein are qualified in their entirety by such reference.

Legal Matters—Litigation

The legality of the securities offered hereby has been passed upon for the Trust by:

XYZ
Attorney at Law
(Address)

There is no litigation pending involving the Trust.

Experts

The Balance Sheet included in this Prospectus has been examined by Deloitte, Haskins & Sells, independent certified public accountants, as set forth in their opinion appearing herein, and has been so included in reliance upon their opinion and upon the authority of that firm as experts in accounting and auditing.

Additional Information

This Prospectus does not contain all the information set forth in the Registration Statement and the exhibits thereto which the Trust has filed with the Securities and Exchange Commission, Washington, D.C. under the Securities Act of 1933, to which Registration Statement reference is hereby made. For further information pertaining to the Trust and the Shares offered hereby, reference is made to the Registration Statement, including the exhibits and the financial statements and notes filed as part thereof. Copies of the exhibits are on file at the office of the Securities and Exchange Commission in Washington, D.C. and may be obtained at rates prescribed by the Commission upon request to the Commission.

The name First National Realty Trust is the designation of the Trustees under a Declaration of Trust dated as of 1 August, 1983, and all persons dealing with First National Realty Trust must look solely to the Trust estate for the enforcement of any claims against First National Realty Trust, as neither the Trustees, officers, agents nor security holders assume any personal liability for obligations entered into on behalf of First National Realty Trust and their respective properties shall not be subject to the claims of any other person in respect of any such liability or obligation.

Opinion of Independent Certified Public Accountants

FIRST NATIONAL REALTY TRUST:

We have examined the balance sheet of FIRST NATIONAL REALTY TRUST [a California real estate investment trust] as of_____. Our examination was made in accordance with generally accepted auditing standards, and accordingly included such tests of the accounting records and such other auditing procedures as we considered necessary in the circumstances.

In our opinion, the accompanying balance sheet presents fairly the financial position of FIRST NATIONAL REALTY TRUST as of _____ in conformity with generally accepted accounting principles.

FIRST NATIONAL REALTY TRUST
BALANCE SHEET
as of
1 August 1983

CASH	$200,000
SHAREHOLDER'S EQUITY:	
Shares of beneficial interest, par value $1 per Share, unlimited authorization; 20,000 Shares issued and outstanding	20,000
Additional paid-in capital	180,000
TOTAL	$200,000

NOTES:

1. First National Realty Trust was organized under the laws of California pursuant to a Declaration of Trust dated 1 August, 1983, and has no operations other than those relating to organizational matters and the sale and issuance of shares of beneficial interest.
2. Reference is made to "The Advisor" elsewhere in this Prospectus regarding the agreement with First National Advisors, Inc., for the services as investment advisor of the Trust.

REGISTRATION INFORMATION
SECTIONS A & B MUST BE COMPLETED BY UNDERWRITER BEFORE THIS SALE WILL BE EFFECTIVE

To be Registered as Follows:

INVESTOR INFORMATION—Section A

Name or Names _____
                          First   Middle   Last

Name or Names _____
Street Address _____
City _____ State _____ Zip _____
Country if not USA _____ Soc. Sec. No. _____
Area Code _____ Telephone No. _____
Check here if previous investment made in this Trust _____

SALESMAN INFORMATION—Section B

Salesman's Name _____
Salesman's Off. Address _____
City _____ State _____ Zip _____
Country if not USA _____ Soc. Sec. No. _____
Area Code _____ Telephone No. _____

UNDERWRITER INFORMATION—Section B

Underwriter Name _____
Underwriter Add. Line _____
Underwriter Add. Line _____
City _____ State _____ Zip _____
Area Code _____ Telephone No. _____ Tax ID NO. _____
    Underwriter Authorized Signature _____

REGISTRATION INFORMATION (continued)

_____ By: _____
                                        Name of Registered Representative
Branch Office: _____

Note: Payment for shares must accompany this Order Form. Make checks payable to: Crocker National Bank, 6301 Beach Blvd., Buena Park, CA 90621, or Security Pacific National Bank, 1633 N. Hacienda Blvd., La Puente, CA 91747. Also, make sure that all items above are complete. The minimum initial order is $500.00 (50 Shares).

ORDER FORM

TO: FIRST NATIONAL REALTY TRUST

Gentlemen:

1. The buyer identified at Section 3 hereby orders the number of shares of beneficial interest ($1.00 par value) First National Realty Trust, a California trust (the "Trust") set forth below at the purchase price of $10.00 per share:
   _____Shares _____ Total purchase price.
2. The undersigned hereby represents that it has heretofore caused a copy of the Prospectus dated _____ to be delivered to the buyer and that the buyer has heretofore acknowledged to the undersigned that he received such Prospectus.
3. The buyer has supplied to the undersigned the following information upon which the Trust may rely in connection with this order:
   a. Name _____
   b. Address _____
      City_____ State_____ Zip Code_____
   c. Social Security or Taxpayer's Identification No. _____
4. All Shares ordered hereby to be owned and registered as follows:
   Name_____ (and) _____
   Street Address_____
   City _____ State _____ Zip Code _____

Check one:
   _____ INDIVIDUAL OWNERSHIP (one signature required)
   _____ JOINT TENANTS WITH RIGHT OF SURVIVORSHIP (one signature required)
   _____ COMMUNITY PROPERTY (one signature required)
   _____ TENANTS IN COMMON (both parties must sign)
   _____ OTHER _____
                            (Specify)
   Dated: _____ _____
                                        Name of Underwriter

ORDER FORM (continued)

To be completed by Underwriter Office Personnel.
Investor Number _____ Underwriter Number _____
Salesman Number _____
New Underwriter   New Branch Office   New Salesman
Check Here _____ Check Here _____ Check Here _____
A = Add
B = Change
C = Delete   Type of Ownership ___ Whslr. _____
No. of Shares _____ Total Amount _____
Received and accepted by: Date _____
DATE: _____ BY: _____

Bibliography

Abbott, Lawrence. *Economics and the Modern World.* 2d ed. New York: Harcourt, Brace and World, 1967.
Accident Investigation and Claims Adjusting. Lessons 1–16. Dallas, Tex.: Universal Schools, 1964.
Anderson, Leland G. *Cal/OSHA Guide for the Construction Industry.* San Francisco: Cal/OSHA Communication Unit, 1981.
Anderson, Ronald A. *Business Law.* 5th ed. Cincinnati, Ohio: South-Western Publishing Company, 1952.
Ball, John E. *Exterior and Interior Trim.* New York: Van Nostrand Reinhold Co., 1975.
Bank Secrecy Act. Corporate Law and Practice #202. New York: Practicing Law Institute, 1976.
Bentel, Frederick K. *Bank Officers' Handbook of Commercial Banking Law.* 4th ed. Boston: Warren, Gorham and Lamont, Inc., 1975.
———. *Bank Officers' Handbook of Commercial Banking Law.* 4th ed. Boston: Warren, Gorham and Lamont, Inc., 1975.
Benton, William R. *Real Estate Investment.* Englewood Cliffs, N.J.: Prentice-Hall, 1971.
Bloodworth, Venia. *Key to Yourself.* Marina del Rey, Calif.: DeVorss and Company, 1950.
Bonny, John B., and Fren, Joseph P. *Handbook of Construction Management and Organization.* New York: Van Nostrand Reinhold Co., 1973.
Buffington, G. N. *Handbook of Member Trusts.* Washington, D.C.: National Association of Real Estate Investment Trusts, Inc., 1974/75.
California Coastal Plan. Sacramento, Calif.: Documents and Publications Branch, 1975.
California Contractors Examination Course. Santa Ana, Calif.: Contractors License Service, 1972.
Childs, John F. *Long Term Financing.* Englewood Cliffs, N.J.: Prentice-Hall, 1961.
Chruder, Herbert J., and Sherman, Arthur W., Jr. *Personnel Management.* 6th ed. Cincinnati, Ohio: Southwestern Publishing Company, 1980.
Claus, George, and Bolander, Karen. *Ecological Sanity.* New York: David McKay Company, Inc., 1977.

Cohen, Irving M. *Electrical Estimating Handbook*. New York: Construction Publishing Company, Inc., 1975.
Corey, E. Raymond, Lovelock, Christopher H., and Ward, Scott. *Problems in Marketing*. 6th ed. New York: McGraw-Hill Book Company, 1981.
Cyr, John E. *Training and Supervising Real Estate Salesmen*. Englewood Cliffs, N.J.: Prentice-Hall, 1973.
Davis, Keith. *Human Behavior at Work: Organizational Behavior*. New York: McGraw-Hill, 1981.
Davis, Lawrence H., ed. *Mobile Homes and Mobile Home Parks*. New York: McGraw-Hill, 1975.
de Betts, Ralph F. *The New Deal's SEC: The Formulative Years*. New York: Columbia University Press, 1964.
Doris, Lillian. *Corporate Treasurers and Controllers Encyclopedia*. Vols. 1–4. Englewood Cliffs, N.J.: Prentice-Hall, 1958.
Doris, Lillian and Friedman, Edith J. *Encyclopedia of Corporate Meetings, Minutes and Resolutions*. Vols. 1–3. Englewood Cliffs, N.J.: Prentice Hall, 1975.
Dresser, Horatio W. *The Quimby Manuscripts*. New York: Julian Press, Inc., 1961.
Dresser, Julius A. *The Philosophy of P. P. Quimby*. Boston, Mass.: George M. Ellis, Printer, 1895.
Fallington, James F., Reed, Harvey B., and McCookle, Julie N. *The College Omnibus*. New York: Harcourt, Brace and Company, 1938.
Fallon, E. B. *The Appraiser Handbook*. Hicksville, N.Y.: Exposition Press, 1975.
Fire and Casualty, Life and Disability Insurance Manual. Los Angeles: State of California Department of Insurance, 1982.
Fox, George. *Amok*. New York: Simon & Schuster, 1978.
Freund, Philip. *The Spy Master*. New York: Ives Washburn, Inc., 1965.
Galeno, Joseph J. *Plumbing Estimating Handbook*. New York: Construction Publishing Company, 1976.
Gilmore, Eugene A., and Wesmuth, William C. *Modern American Law*. Course of Study. 16 vols. Chicago: Blackstone Institute, Inc., 1914.
Gross, Martin L. *The Doctors*. New York: Random House, 1966.
Heldman, Gladys M. *The Harmonetics Investigation*. New York: Crown Publishers, Inc., 1979.
Henry, William R. *Managerial Economics*. 4th ed. Plano, Tex.: Business Publications, Inc., 1963.
Holmes, Ernest. *How to Change Your Life*. Los Angeles: Science of Mind, 1987.
Horan, James D. *The Seat of Power*. New York: Crown Publishers, Inc., 1965.
Hotema, Hilton. *Secret of Regeneration*. Mokelumne Hill, Calif.: Health Research, 1963.
Hudson, Thomson Jay. *Physical Manifestations and Philosophy of Christ*. Salinas, Calif.: Hudson-Cohan Publishing 1893.

———. *The Laws of Psychic Phenomena.* Salinas, Calif.: Hudson-Cohan Publishing, 1893.

Hurst, James Willard. *The Legal History of Money.* Lincoln, Nebr.: University of Nebraska Press, 1973.

Jackson, Bruce. *In the Life.* New York: Holt, Rinehart and Winston, 1972.

James, Marjorie D., ed. *Portfolio of Accounting Systems for Small and Medium-Size Businesses.* Vols. 1 and 2. Englewood Cliffs, N.J.: Prentice-Hall, Inc., 1968.

Johnson, James E., and Balsigor, David W. *Beyond Defeat.* Garden City, New York: Doubleday and Company, Inc., 1978.

Kellett, Michael. *High Intensity Memory Power.* New York: Sterling Publishing Company, Inc., 1980.

Kennedy, Susan Easterbrook. *The Banking Crisis of 1933.* Lexington: University Press of Kentucky, 1973.

Loomis, Evarts G. *Healing for Everyone.* New York: Hawthorne Books, Inc., 1975.

Mancuso, Anthony. *How to Form Your Own California Corporation.* Berkeley, Calif.: Nolo Press, 1977.

Mauer, David A., and Vogel, Victor H. *Narcotics and Narcotics Addiction.* 3rd ed. Springfield, Ill.: Charles C. Thomas Publisher, 1967.

McCullough, David. *The Path between the Seas.* New York: Simon & Schuster, 1977.

McInery, Ralph. *The Priest.* New York: Harper and Row, 1973.

Michener, James A. *The Covenant.* New York: Random House, 1980.

Moffatt, James. *The Bible: A New Translation.* New York: Harper and Brothers Publishers, 1922.

Mooney, Michael M. *The Ministry of Culture.* New York: Wyndham Books, 1980.

Mullin, Ray C., and Smith, Robert L. *Electrical Wiring Commercial.* New York: Van Nostrand Reinhold Company, 1977.

Murphy, Joseph. *Your Infinite Power to Be Rich.* West Nyack, N.J.: Parker Publishing Company, 1966.

———. *Love is Freedom.* Marina del Rey, Calif.: Book Graphics, 1965.

———. *Infinite Power for Richer Living.* West Nyack, N.Y.: Parker Publishing Company, Inc., 1979.

———. *Collected Essays.* Marina del Rey, Calif.: DeVorss and Company, 1987.

———. *Songs of God.* Marina del Rey, Calif.: DeVorss and Company, 1979.

———. *Pray Your Way Through It.* Marina del Rey, Calif.: DeVorss and Company, 1958.

———. *Living without Strain.* Marina del Rey, Calif.: DeVorss and Company, 1959.

———. *How to Use the Laws of Mind.* Marina del Rey, Calif.: DeVorss and Company, 1980.

Naisbitt, John. *Megatrends.* New York: Warner Books, Inc., 1982.

Newkirk, R. and R. *Introduce Yourself to Securities*. Indianapolis: The Research and Review Service, 1982.

Nickerson, Clarence B. *Accounting Handbooks for Non-Accountants*. Boston: Cohners Books International, Inc., 1975.

O'Brien, James J. *Construction Inspection Handbook*. New York: Van Nostrand Reinhold Company, 1974.

Office of Civil Defense, Department of Defense. *In Time of Emergency*. Washington, D.C.: U.S. Printing Office, 1968.

Oldenbourg, Zoe. *The Heirs of the Kingdom*. New York: Pantheon Books, 1971.

Olenich, Arnold J. *Managing the Company Tax Function*. Englewood Cliffs, N.J.: Prentice-Hall, 1976.

O'Malia, Thomas J. *Banker's Guide to Financial Statements*. Boston: Bankers Publishing Company, 1976.

Orange County Progress Report. Vol. 23. Santa Ana, Calif.: County of Orange, California, 1986/87.

Osborn, Alex. *Make Up Your Mind*. New York: Charles Scribners Sons, 1952.

Reskin, Melvin A., and Sakai, Hiroshi. *Modern Real Estate and Mortgage Forms*. Boston, Mass.: Warren, Gorman & Lamont, 1973.

Russell, Robert A. *The Quickest Way to Everything Good*. Denver: The Shrine of the Healing Presence, 1914.

Sederberg, Arelo. *The Power Players*. New York: William Morrow and Company, 1980.

Seltz, David D. *How to Get Started in Your Own Franchise Business*. New York: Farnsworth Publishing Company, Inc., 1967.

Sherwood, J. F., and Culey, Roy T. *Auditing Theory and Procedure*. Cincinnati, Ohio: South-Western Publishing Company, 1939.

Smith, R. Harris. *OSS*. Berkeley: University of California Press, 1972.

Troward, Judge Thomas. *The Hidden Power*. 16th ed. New York: Dodd, Mead and Company, 1921.

―――. *The Creative Process in the Individual*. London: L. N. Fowler and Company, Ltd., 1910.

―――. *Bible Mystery and Bible Meaning*. New York: Dodd, Mead and Company, 1913.

―――. *The Law and the Word*. New York: Dodd, Mead and Company, 1917.

Turner, John R. *Modern Business*. Course of Study, Vol. 28. New York: Alexander Hamilton Institute, 1959.

West's Annotated California Codes. Sections 9,000–24,999; 25,000 to end. Official California Corporation Code Classifications. St. Paul, Minn.: West Publishing Company, 1977.

Wiley, Robert J. *Real Estate Investment Analysis and Strategy*. New York: John Wiley and Sons, 1977.